The Spring
Assembly Book

The Spring Assembly Book

REDVERS BRANDLING

SIMON & SCHUSTER
EDUCATION

First published in 1993 in Great Britain by
Simon & Schuster Education
Campus 400, Maylands Avenue
Hemel Hempstead, Herts HP2 7EZ

British Library Cataloguing in Publication Data is
available on request from the British Library

ISBN 0 7501 0607 7

Set in 11/13pt Times by
Columns Design and Production
Services Ltd, Reading
Printed in Great Britain by
T.J. Press (Padstow) Ltd, Padstow, Cornwall.

Contents

Acknowledgements   *page* viii

Introduction   ix

Section A: complete assemblies   1

January

1	This month	3
2	The hero	5
3	Home Sweet Home?	8
4	Good value?	10
5	A helping paw	12
6	The prince	14
7	The weekend	17
8	St Nathalan	19
9	Here he comes	22
10	Avalanche!	24
11	It will be all right	27
12	The cut	29
13	Be prepared	32
14	A dog's life	35
15	Peace and quiet	37
16	Our daily bread	39
17	Is it worth it?	41

February

18	The recipe	44
19	What's inside?	46
20	Judy	48
21	This month	51
22	Patience	53
23	Pass it on	55
24	Rescue	57
25	We need a king!	60

26 Two's company   62
27 The plot   65
28 Teamwork   67
29 The man whom everybody liked   70
30 A great discovery   72
31 In a garden in Medina   75
32 Winkie   77
33 Doing what is best   79
34 Welcome to a stranger   81

March

35 Guard my treasure   84
36 More!   86
37 This month   88
38 One hot Australian day   91
39 Tell the truth   94
40 Not quite perfect   96
41 The healing of the blind man   99
42 A cause for concern   101
43 The idols   104
44 Fame   106
45 Thanks, driver!   109
46 The lost sheep   111
47 The Ethel Langton story   113
48 All change   116
49 Hero Wong   118
50 What is your opinion?   120
51 I need some help   122

April

52 A good joke   125
53 The second chance   128
54 Is that really what you want?   130
55 This month   133
56 Mother Samwell   136
57 Ruswarp the faithful   138
58 Don't leave it too late   140
59 Learning a lesson   143
60 Don't count your chickens before they're hatched 145

Section B: class assemblies linked to significant times in the term   149

1   The best time is now   151
2   Fun for all   156
3   What was it like?   161
4   Report from Jerusalem   166
5   Food for thought   171

Section C: anniversaries, facts, fancies, anecdotes, religious notes for every day of the spring term   177

January   179
February   186
March   191
April   197

Section D: assemblies linked by theme   201

Animals, Concern, Courage, Environment,
Faith, Friendship, Guidance, Heroes and Heroines, Home,
Journeys, Living Together, Ourselves, Senses,
Those Who Help Us

Section E: the stories   205

Folk stories, myths, legends
True stories
Religious stories
Original or contemporary stories

Section F: National Curriculum cross-references   207

Art
English
Geography
History
Mathematics
Music
Physical Education
Science
Technology

Section G: resources   211

Acknowledgements

I am, as always, grateful to the staff and children of Dewhurst St Mary School, Cheshunt. They have been a receptive audience for all the material in this book, and a source of both inspiration and information with their own presentations.

The material supplied to schools from Save the Children and the Christian Education Movement has been of great value. Of the many anthologies referred to, *Folk Tales of India* and *Folk Tales of the World* (both published by Sterling) have been especially valuable.

It should also be mentioned that some of the stories in this book have been used, heard and re-adapted several times in assemblies. In consequence their original sources are not remembered and if this has unwittingly caused the infringement of copyright, the author apologises and will correct this omission in future editions, if notified.

Introduction

'Effective assembly occasions take a great deal of time to prepare.'[1]

'Assemblies must contain a sense of expectancy, a willingness to co-operate, some unity between those present by reason of shared experiences or common values.'[2]

'In achieving this meaningful act . . . other means . . . are valid . . . stories and readings; dance and drama; prayer/meditation; creative silence; songs/hymns/music; sacred/secular readings; artefacts and natural materials; children's contributions; visual aids.'[3]

[1] *Themes for Assembly*, S Brimer (Blackie and Son)
[2] *First School Religious Education*, T and G Copley (SCM Press)
[3] *Collective Worship in Hertfordshire*, Guidance for schools.

These quotations effectively reinforce what all those who take even an occasional assembly already know. Apart from its being a mandatory daily requirement, the primary school assembly should at all times be well presented, thoughtful, reflective, and involve the children. For ever-increasingly busy Heads and teachers it is therefore an extremely demanding task.

This is the second of three books comprising material for the autumn, spring and summer terms. It seeks to provide constructive, practical help for a complete spring term of assemblies.

It begins with a series of ready-made assemblies for each month – seventeen each for January, February and March, and nine for April. This gives a total of sixty assemblies which are 'instant' in that they provide an introduction, story, suggested hymn and prayer. They also, however, contain sections on 'Information for the teacher' and 'National Curriculum cross-curricular reference.' The use of these will hopefully enhance each assembly and, as with any ready-made material, reflection and preparation beforehand add enormously to its potential.

The second section in the book contains a number of class

assemblies. Once again these are prepared in a detailed manner – aims, materials required, calendar location, numbers involved, preparation, information, presentation – and contain a variety of playscripts. The latter are reproduced in large print so that they can be used for photocopying and group involvement.

Section C contains an anniversary, fact, fancy or anecdote for every day in the spring term. Many of these are ideal starting material for other assemblies and interspersed with them are notes referring to ready-made assemblies elsewhere in the book. Where this is the case links of ideas or themes offer further expansion possibilities.

For teachers who do not wish to use the assemblies chronologically and prefer a thematic approach, Sections D and E aim to help in this context. Section D groups assemblies into popular primary school themes – *animals*, *concern*, *courage*, etc. Section E links the assemblies by their source – *folk*, *true*, *religious*, *original*, etc.

Section F acknowledges that many teachers now feel that assembly material should be linked to other areas of the National Curriculum. This is done here by identifying other National Curriculum subjects and linking assemblies to them where appropriate.

The final section in the book provides details of resources.

Redvers Brandling

Section A
Complete assemblies

January

1 This month

Introduction

January is the month we say 'Happy New Year' to each other. We think about new beginnings – and learning from our mistakes of the last year. January is also the month when it seems as if winter is going on for ever . . . but it isn't.

This month

January is often the coldest month of the year, but there are strange contrasts during this month.

When there is frost and snow there are problems both in town and country. Roads become dangerous, pipes freeze and stored potatoes have to be protected with straw or even heaters. Small birds are in danger when it is cold. This is because the surface area of a small bird is large compared with the rest of its body. Surfaces lose warmth quickly so the bird's body gets cold quickly. We can help by putting out plenty of food on the bird table. When it eats, the bird gets both heat and energy from the food.

At the same time, however, January does promise the end of winter. If you look carefully at the tips of branches you can see that leaf buds are already beginning to swell, and yellow hazel catkins start to come out during this month. Masses of starlings start to swirl about the sky just before it gets dark, and if there is a really sunny day during the month squirrels start to appear more often. The first baby lambs are born in January. Flowers are very few but yellow gorse can be seen on commons and hillsides and the first snowdrops are starting to peep through.

The first Monday after the Twelve Days of Christmas used to be a day when ploughmen all over the country had parties and went from door to door collecting money. The reason for this was that they were marking the end of their holidays with a special occasion and preparing to start work again. You might think of this when you see tractors and ploughs cutting their furrows through the bare fields.

Information for the teacher

1 Quite a few schools have tailor's dummies on which school uniforms or other costumes are displayed. In this assembly it would be useful to dress up the dummy for the assembly in what seems the most appropriate clothing for the month. As the month progresses, the children can reflect on the appropriateness of this clothing to the prevailing weather.
2 Primary school children are fascinated by the line of thought that January is named after the Roman god Janus, and that the Latin word '*jauna*' means 'door'. Thus we move through the door into the new year, leaving disappointments behind and striving for better things to come.
3 The 6th of the month is the celebration of the Feast of the Epiphany in the Christian Church. This is the time when the three kings supposedly arrived in Bethlehem.
4 Bearing in mind the idea that January offers the opportunity to 'turn over a new leaf', reference to the Bible might be useful in locating passages which suggest admirable virtues. Possible references might be: Matthew 15, 29–31 for determination; Luke 16, 19–31 for concern and kindness; Romans 12, 1–5 for unselfishness.

Hymn suggestion

Come and Praise Vol 2 'It's a new day' No 106

Prayer

Let us bow our heads and think this morning of January in Britain. It is a time when, beneath the cold and darkness, preparations are being made for new life.

Let us think about our own lives and ways in which we can try to be more helpful and considerate people.

National Curriculum cross-curricular reference

Science is an obvious link via themes such as cold, growth, beginnings. When there is snow the examining of domestic animal tracks can spark off fascinating work in Science, History and English.

To give an example: in the Verulamium Museum in St Albans, Hertfordshire, there is a clay tile estimated as being two thousand years old and containing clear dog's paw marks. Such a 'starter' offers many possibilities: life as a Roman dog; what would that dog think if reborn today?

2 The hero

Introduction

Have you got a hero? Do you admire someone for their talent, or a skill, or any actions? Is there anybody about whom you would like to say, 'I wish I was like that'? This morning's story is about an unusual hero.

Story

'Those monkeys are too noisy,' said the king to one of his ministers. 'I'm going to get rid of them for ever.'

'Yes, your majesty,' replied the minister, bowing low.

Then he listened carefully to the king's plans.

A few days later the king and the minister, together with a squad of soldiers armed with spears and bows and arrows, set out for the huge trees where all the monkeys lived. Several eyes watched their progress.

Within minutes the movement of the soldiers was being reported to the leader of the monkeys.

'They're coming – lots of men with weapons! They're going to surround the tree and kill us all – I know it!'

'Keep calm, keep calm,' said the monkey leader. 'I know a way in which we can escape.'

Meanwhile the king and his soldiers had reached the tree. The soldiers began to push their way through the bushes and soon the tree was surrounded.

'When you're all in position I'll give the order to fire,' said the king. 'Then we'll be rid of these nuisances for ever.'

The leader of the monkeys heard the movement and voices as he worked desperately to save his friends. Running alongside the great tree was a river, and on the other side of the river was another tree with great creepers hanging down from it.

'Now, I can jump the river,' thought the monkey leader, 'and then swing back on one of those creepers. If I tie it to this tree all the monkeys can use it as a bridge and escape to the other side.'

So, as the soldiers moved into position, the monkey leader crossed the river, chose the longest creeper, and swung back to the home tree with it . . . but there was a snag. The creeper was just not quite long enough to reach between the two trees.

'No problem,' thought the leader. 'I'll make up the distance with my own body.' So, with one arm hanging onto the tree and the other arm outstretched to grip the creeper, the monkey leader was suspended in space – the last link of his bridge.

Now things started to happen quickly. Seeing their escape route ready and hearing their leader's instructions, the monkeys began to pour over the bridge to safety. Furious at the thought of them escaping, the king called out to his soldiers, 'Fire – before they all escape!'

Struggling to get their bows ready, the soldiers managed to get a few arrows off but none of the monkeys was hit. Then a terrible thing happened.

The last monkey in the home tree was one who for years had been jealous of the leader. He was filled with envy and hatred and suddenly he saw the chance to get rid of his rival and become leader himself.

Leaping from the tree, he crashed feet first into the tired and aching back of the monkey leader, smashing him away from the tree. With a terrible cry of pain the monkey leader fell to the ground while his evil rival grabbed the creeper and swung away to safety.

From the ground the king had seen all this happen. As the monkey leader crashed to the ground, he called out to his men, 'Stop firing! Stop firing at once.'

Pushing desperately through the bushes, the king reached the monkey leader. He saw at once that the leader was in great pain and dying.

'A doctor!' cried the king. 'To the palace at once and get a doctor.'

It was no use. The monkey leader died as the group of men stood round him. The king spoke with bowed head to them all.

'Never in my life have I seen a braver action than this. This monkey will be buried as if he were a king and the story of his courage will be told to all children and never forgotten.'

Information for the teacher

1 This is an adaptation from an old Buddhist story from the *Jataka* tales. The king was the King of Benares and the evil monkey was called Devadatta. This story is an excellent one for reflecting the Four Noble Truths of the Buddhist religion. These are:
   • suffering is a part of life;
   • selfishness is the cause of suffering;
   • if selfishness is overcome then suffering will stop;
   • following the 'eightfold path' towards perfection will bring suffering to an end.
   The Buddha also told his followers that three of the greatest selfish evils were greed, hatred and laziness.
2 A possible calendar link is with Education Sunday which is held in some Christian churches during this month. Buddhism is very much concerned with teaching. '*Dharma*' is the name given to the Buddha's teaching.

Hymn suggestion

Come and Praise Vol 2 'All the animals' No 80

Prayer

Let us bow our heads and think this morning about some of the advice given in the words of the Buddhist religion: 'Mules and horses and elephants are excellent when trained, but more excellent is the man who has trained himself.'

National Curriculum cross-curricular reference

Geography is a strong link: areas of the world in which Buddhism is prominent could be located.

The idea and effectiveness of the swinging creeper could be examined more thoroughly in Science. This story could also be strongly linked to English – there are very good discussion possibilities and it is an ideal medium for drama.

There is also a strong sense of 'movement' about this story. Many teachers will be familiar with how the feeling of movement is captured so effectively in musical terms in 'The Sorcerer's Apprentice'. There could be a case for some musical improvisation and experimentation in connection with the story.

3   Home Sweet Home?

Introduction

Let's suppose that you've had 'one of those days' at school – you've had an argument with your best friend, got your maths all wrong, you got drenched on the way home, you're freezing . . . where do you most want to be? Now listen to this morning's story.

Story

Geoff was excited. He had been away for the weekend with a party from school. They had been at a computer centre and it had been great, right from the Friday night when they got there. He'd missed home though, and now the coach was turning down the familiar street he thought how glad he would be to be back.

'Anybody want to be out here?' called out the coach driver.

'Yes, please,' replied Mr Clarke. 'This is your place, isn't it, Geoff?'

'Yes, sir,' answered Geoff, looking to see if there were any lights on in the flat on the second floor.

The bus stopped and Geoff dragged his haversack off the step and slung it over his shoulder.

'Bye, Geoff,' called one or two of his friends, and Mr Clarke gave him a friendly wave.

'I can't wait to tell them all about it,' thought Geoff as he pushed through the front door and began to climb up the stairs to his flat. When he reached the landing he pressed the switch and the lights came on over the staircase. He noticed that the door to his flat – number 4 – was standing slightly open.

'Funny,' he thought, and pushed it open.

'I'm home,' he called in a loud voice. 'I'm . . .'

It was then that he got his first shock. The front room was empty – no furniture, no carpet, no TV, and all the pictures gone from the walls.

'Mum —' Geoff called out, in a faltering voice. 'Mum . . . Dad . . .'

Dropping his bags on the floor, he charged through the flat like a madman. 'Mum . . . Dad . . . MUM! DAD!'

The flat was empty. There was no sign of his mother or father. Everything else had gone too. Even the fridge was empty.

Geoff thought he was having some horrible nightmare. He couldn't believe what he saw around him. He was hungry and thirsty and lonely, and his home – had gone.

Information for the teacher

1 On occasion, assemblies which come under the banner of 'Causes for Concern' are extremely effective. This is one of them and it is based on the true story of Frank, an American boy who returned to his home in New York after a trip and found just this situation. He had to survive living on the streets. (The source of the story was *LINX*, that excellent magazine produced by the Education Unit of Save The Children Fund, 17 Grove Lane, London SE5 8RD.)
2 Frank's mother and stepfather had simply fallen on hard times and left him while he was away at camp. He had no inkling such a thing was going to happen.
3 It is estimated that 2,000–3,000 young people sleep rough in central London every night, many through no fault of their own.
4 The poignancy of this story is emphasised by the following comment by a child of refugee parents who were still with her: 'Yes, we have a home, but no house to put round it.'

Hymn suggestion

Come and Praise Vol 2 'Sad, puzzled eyes' No 74

Prayer

Dear God,
Let us think this morning of those children who, wherever they are in the world, are without a home and all that means. Let us think of those children who are lonely and abandoned. Let us pray that they do not lose hope and find the love that everyone needs. Amen.

National Curriculum cross-curricular reference

Apart from the many and wide-ranging RE issues which this story promotes, it is also the sort of emotive material which generates considerable discussion points in English. Similarly, there is great scope here for follow-up writing in the 'what happened next' theme.

4 Good value?

Introduction

What do you think is the greatest treasure you have? (*You may seek answers if you wish*.) Sometimes what seems a treasure to one person is certainly not to another. This morning's story really makes us think about 'good value'.

Story

Ali was fat. He was also very rich and very boastful. He had got rich by leading his camels from town to town and selling rich silks, ivory, ebony, coral, rubies and fine-quality linen clothes. He had got fat by sitting beside open fires in towns like Damascus and Jerusalem and boasting about the quality of his goods and how much money he made on every trip.

Ali liked talking, but he wasn't so good at listening. He certainly didn't want to listen to another merchant telling everybody about how rich and successful *he* was. But that's what happened.

Ali's arrival in a desert town had coincided with the arrival of Achmed. Now, Achmed wasn't fat, but in every other respect he was like Ali – rich, hard-working and boastful.

The group of listeners who had gathered around the blazing fire listened with a mixture of awe, interest and disbelief as the two merchants held forth.

'Best trip I ever had to old Jerusalem,' said Ali loudly. 'Bought a sack of coloured silk from Damascus and I couldn't sell it fast enough. I was up half the night counting the money I made on that trip.'

Achmed gave a superior smile. 'Silk, bales of silk, bah! That's not really a money-earner. What you want is precious stones. Now there's a chance for a real profit . . .'

Ali interrupted. 'Oh, I've carried plenty of precious stones in my time too. But of course only the biggest and the best.'

The crowd round the fire gasped as Ali reached into the folds of his cloak and brought out a huge pearl. The firelight sparkled as Ali twisted it round in his fingers. 'A merchant who has a load of pearls like this with him has nothing to worry about, nothing at all. His future is guaranteed.'

Achmed was just about to go one better when a small and rather poor looking man at the back of the group spoke, in a harsh, cutting voice.

'Rubbish,' he said.

Everyone turned to look at him: Ali and Achmed eyed him indignantly; everyone else waited with expectation.

'I was once a merchant like you two, with one of the biggest camel trains ever seen on the desert. Richer and richer I got and, on one final trip, I decided to make myself more money than I could ever have imagined. My father and brothers decided to join me on the trip. We filled all the camel bags with jewels and precious stones. Everything else was abandoned so we could travel fast and light.

'We were a day out on our journey when the worst sandstorm in living memory blew up in the desert. In minutes we were lost. We struck camp, intending to get back to our route when everything had blown over – but it didn't. We had hundreds of precious stones, but no food or water. Gradually my father and two brothers died, and then the servants, and then the camels.

'How I survived I don't know, but a search party came across me more dead than alive – and I've never been the same man since.'

Sweeping his cloak round his skeleton-like frame, the speaker got up and left the fireside group. There was silence. What Ali and Achmed had to say didn't seem important any more.

Information for the teacher

1 An ancient city's gate was one of its focal points. Here was a market place, and here justice was meted out and jobs sought and given. (Bible references: Matthew 20, 3; Ruth 4.)
2 Linen was a very prized material in the East, being both fresher and cleaner than wool. Clothes of purple and scarlet were particularly expensive because the dye for these could only be obtained from the juices of a shellfish caught near the Phoenician port of Tyre.
3 The great caravan routes ranged over the Sinai desert, alongside the Dead Sea, and from Egypt through the passes of Mount Carmel.
4 Camels are mentioned frequently in the Bible. (Genesis; Exodus; 1 Kings 10 refers to the Queen of Sheba's camel train of gifts to Solomon; 11 Kings 8, 9 refers to the forty-camel train of gifts for Elisha.) Camels were very valuable because they were durable and cheap to feed. They would even eat thistles. Reaching maturity at sixteen years, they lived to an old age.

5 There are two useful calendar links with this story. The 6th is the date linked with the journey of the Magi. On the 24th the 'value' angle could be developed. It was on this date in 1848 that gold was first discovered in California, leading to the Gold Rush and many tragedies.

Hymn suggestion

Come and Praise Vol 1 'The best gift' No 59

Prayer

Let us think this morning about the value of things. How precious is food to the starving and water to the thirsty; a home to those who have none; a friend to those who are lonely.

Let us have the sense to value the really important things in life and always to appreciate our own good fortune.

National Curriculum cross-curricular reference

Both History and Geography are well served here. Children could research a variety of topics: old caravan trails, reasons for their existence and location, modern counterparts, etc.

Maths could be incorporated in the trading aspect and there is scope for some unusual and dramatic work in Art — silhouettes, sunsets in the desert, etc.

Drama could also be used to portray the story and imaginative follow-ups.

5 A helping paw

Introduction

Some wild animals are very frightening. For instance, how would you like to come face to face with a lion . . . ?

Story

The afternoon light was fading as the group of monks sat in the chapel. One was reading aloud while the others were still and quiet, listening. Suddenly they were aware of movement at the back of the chapel. Turning, they saw that limping slowly down the aisle was an enormous lion!

There were gasps and cries and, in an undignified scuffle, the monks bundled past each other – all trying to get out of the chapel before the lion reached them. All, that is, except a monk called Jerome. He saw the lion too, but he took the trouble to look at it a little more closely.

'He's hurt,' Jerome muttered to himself as the lion limped nearer. Getting up from his seat, he turned and walked slowly towards the lion.

'You're hurt, old friend,' he said in a quiet voice. 'You're hurt. How can I help?'

As if he understood, and without pausing in his limping stride, the lion came right up to the monk and lifted up his front paw.

'Ah, this is the problem, is it?' said Jerome. 'Well, let's have a close look at it.'

Bending down, the monk examined the paw carefully. It was swollen and badly cut. 'Looks as if you've torn that on some thorns,' murmured Jerome. 'It needs bathing and some ointment on it and in a few days it will be as good as new.'

The lion followed Jerome as the monk set about treating its paw. Within a few days it had healed properly. By this time the other monks had got over their fear of the creature because he went about the monastery almost as a pet.

'Now,' said Jerome one day when the lion was completely cured, 'we must think about our friend the lion. We must find him work to do which is useful and suited to him. Have you any suggestions?'

'I've got one,' said one monk straight away. 'You know we've got that donkey to carry wood for our fires? Well, when we're out with him we're always scared some fierce creature is going to attack. Now if he had a guard . . .'

'Excellent,' replied Jerome, 'excellent.'

And so it came about that the lion worked every day protecting the donkey from harm and making sure that the monks got plenty of wood for their fires.

Information for the teacher

1 The theme of hasty reactions to animals could be developed by reflecting on a very different story. This is that of the prince who came home and found his baby's cot covered in blood, with his dog covered in blood too. Suspecting the worst, he slew his dog

immediately, only to find that it had dragged the baby to safety and then fought off the attacking animal which had sought to kill them both.

2 A possibly useful calendar link here is that Gerald Durrell was born on 7th January 1925. He founded the Wildlife Preservation Trust.

Hymn suggestion

Come and Praise Vol 2 'All the animals' No 80

Prayer

> Make us worthy, Lord,
> To care for each other
> And for all living creatures.
>
> Give us courage, Lord,
> To give help when it is needed
> In difficult or frightening circumstances.
>
> Give us faith, Lord,
> That you will guide us
> And make our efforts worthwhile.
>
> Amen.

National Curriculum cross-curricular reference

Lions could be the starting point for a scientific investigation of some wild animals — habits, habitats, food, behaviour, attributes, etc. 'Overcoming fear' is a subject which can provoke good discussion and descriptive writing based on the children's own experience.

6 The prince

Introduction

We all want people to like us. When they don't, however, we tend to say things like: 'What's the matter with him?' Perhaps we ought to say: 'What's the matter with me?' This morning's story tells of a prince long ago . . .

Story

Father and son stood in an upper room in the palace. For as far as they could see, in every direction, was land which they ruled because they were a king and a prince.

'Look well, my son,' said the king, brushing a tired hand across his forehead. 'I am an old man and I will soon be dead. Then you will be king.'

'Yes, father,' said the prince worriedly. He knew his father was a wise and caring king who was loved by his thousands of loyal subjects. 'But,' he went on, 'the people know you. They know you are just and have tried to improve their lives. They admire your wisdom and respect your decisions. How can I even hope to get them on my side, like you?'

'Think about it,' said the old king quietly. 'Think about it.'

The prince did think about it. When he had done this he decided that the only way to get the respect of his subjects was for them to know who he was.

He sent for the commander of the army.

'Prepare a troop of your finest soldiers,' he said. 'I am going to ride with them throughout the length and breadth of the land. Then the people will see what their new king looks like.'

A special troop of soldiers was drawn up. They were the pick of the army – big, fierce looking, well armed and warlike. When they rode, the sound of their horses' hooves was like rolls of thunder. The prince set off with his soldiers.

Things didn't work out as he had planned. When the people in villages and towns saw the clouds of dust and the galloping horsemen, they were frightened. They didn't bother to wait to see what it was all about. Instead they fled, and hid, until the soldiers moved on. The prince was distraught.

'Father,' he said when he returned home, 'I can't get to know your subjects. They run away before I can even see them, never mind talk to them.' He explained to the wise old king what he had done.

The king nodded. 'But you want to win their confidence, not destroy it. Think, my son, think.'

So the prince thought long and hard again. Then he came to a decision. Working day and night, he called learned men from the farthest parts of the kingdom and learnt to be a doctor. Then he set out again.

Wherever he travelled this time he gave freely of his time and skills. His reputation went before him and soon, on arriving at a new town, he would find a meal and a bed waiting for him. He got to know the problems of many of his people and he spoke with thousands of them.

Finally, the old king died and the young prince became the new king. After a brief period of sadness there was great rejoicing. The people felt that they knew their new ruler and that he would rule with wisdom, care and concern. They were right.

Information for the teacher

1 A useful calendar link with the medical side of this story is with Marie Curie who was born on 7th November 1867. Born Maria Sklodovska in Warsaw, she went to Paris to study when she was twenty-four. There she met and married Pierre Curie, a scientist. They discovered that radium was of great value in curing certain diseases. Pierre died in 1906, Marie in 1934 – from the effects of the radioactive substance which had helped so many other people.
2 The 'wisdom' aspect of the story could be expanded to include such people as Solomon, Confucius, Socrates, the Buddha, Guru Nanak. In all cases, reflection on the 'wisdom' aspect would involve comparisons between the characters and their situations.
3 Another useful anniversary is 24th January – the feast day of St Francis de Sales. A brilliant and wealthy scholar, he was expected to become a senator in the French Parliament. Instead he gave up these ambitions and became a priest. As such he always had time for individuals and those in need. He became Bishop of Geneva and died in 1622.

Hymn suggestion

Come and Praise Vol 1 'The wise may bring their learning' No 64

Prayer

Let us pray this morning that those people who are important in guiding our lives are given the wisdom and concern to do it well. Let us give thanks for those people in the past who have set such fine examples of caring for others.

National Curriculum cross-curricular reference

Some useful work could be done in History in examining the qualities which make good rulers, and discussing some good examples from the past. This story is also a very suitable one for drama, so this aspect of English could be followed up.

7 The weekend

Introduction

Sometimes in our lives we meet people for a very short period of time. How they remember us often depends upon how we behaved that time. . .

Story

This is a true story. It is about a family, and a young woman who had recently become a widow.

'We'll go away for the weekend – it's not every day I get a new job,' said Mum.

'All right,' replied Dad. 'The kids will love that. But where will we go?'

'As a matter of fact I've already booked somewhere,' Mum went on. 'I saw an advert in the evening paper. It sounds like a nice house down by the sea near Brighton.'

'Yippee!' cried Wayne, Julie and Lynn when they heard the news.

Meanwhile, in 'the nice house by the sea', Barbara Jackson was worried. Her husband had died six months ago and she had decided to rent out part of her house to holidaymakers so that she could earn a living. Now her first guests were coming for a weekend – a mum, dad, and three children. How would she cope? Could she give them enough food? Would they mess up the bedrooms?

On Friday night Barbara met Geoffrey and Thelma Simpson and Wayne, Julie and Lynn. From the start it was a great weekend for everybody. Geoffrey and Thelma loved the house, the kids loved the games room in the cellar and they all found Barbara and her Great Dane, Alphonse, good company.

'From my point of view, it's just a great relief,' thought Barbara. 'They're such nice people and they're obviously enjoying themselves.'

Sunday afternoon came round all too quickly.

'Go and get the car sorted out – I'll pay the bill,' said Geoffrey Simpson, and Thelma went outside to pack the car.

Soon, after the farewells, the family were on their way back to London. But an hour after Barbara had waved them off, after tidying up, she made an unpleasant discovery.

'How could I?' she said to herself. 'I've charged them for only one room instead of two. Now, instead of making a small profit, I've lost money I could ill afford. Oh dear . . . well, they must be laughing about it. I suppose I've learnt an expensive lesson.'

She had just finished giving Alphonse his tea when there was a knock on the front door. Opening it, Barbara found Thelma Simpson standing there. 'We got talking about the bill on our journey home and we realised you must have made a mistake – so we've come back to pay you what we owe you.'

'But . . . you must have been nearly halfway home,' gasped Barbara.

'Perhaps – but after such a lovely weekend we couldn't let you think we'd cheat you in any way. We just had to come back straight away.'

Minutes later the Simpsons were on their way again. As she waved once more, Barbara's head was full of thoughts. 'If I have ten thousand guests – I'll never forget the Simpsons,' she smiled to herself.

Information for the teacher

1 A nice little anecdote to use in conjunction with this story is the derivation of the word 'sincere'. Marble craftsmen of long ago tricked customers by putting melted wax in flaws in the marble. The more reputable of them gave customers a guarantee saying their work was not fraudulent in this way. The guarantee said SINE CERA (in Latin this meant 'without [*sine*] wax [*cera*]'). From this we get the word 'sincere'.

2 One possible calendar link for this story is the 8th of the month. This was the date in 1941 that Lord Baden Powell died. His insistence on 'honourable' behaviour was one of the keystones of the Boy Scout movement and, later, of the Girl Guides.

Hymn suggestion

Come and Praise Vol 2 'Make us worthy, Lord' No 94

Prayer

Dear God,
Help us to be honest enough to admit our own mistakes. Give us the strength to be honest when it is easier to tell a lie or say nothing. Help us to be honest at all times in both word and deed.
Amen.

National Curriculum cross-curricular reference

There is plenty of scope for English is this theme. Both discussion and written work on lies is useful – lying to gain, 'white lies', lying to protect, etc.

The theme could be expanded in RE because obviously honesty is a quality advocated in all religions.

8 St Nathalan

Introduction

Have you ever done something wrong at home and known that your father and mother have been annoyed at you? (*Pause for answers.*) Have you known, even though they haven't said anything, when they have forgiven you? (*Pause for responses.*) This morning's story is about a man who found he'd been forgiven in a most amazing way.

Story

St Nathalan was a man who felt that helping others was the most important thing in his life. At one time a terrible famine swept over the land where he was living. People were starving and desperate.
    'What can we do?'
    'How can we survive?'
    'Don't worry,' said Nathalan. 'I'm sure we'll get a crop if we sow some of that fine sand this spring.'

'Sand? Sand?!'

'You must be mad. How can we get a crop from sand?'

'You'll see,' said Nathalan, and he got busy with his sowing.

Sure enough, at harvest time a rich crop rose from the ground just waiting to be collected in. Then disaster struck. A terrible storm raged over the countryside and destroyed the entire crop.

Nathalan was flabbergasted – and completely lost his temper. For days he cursed everything and everybody and behaved very badly. Then, as suddenly as it had started, his bad temper left him. When it did he felt more ashamed than he had ever been in his life before.

'After the way I behaved, how can I possibly claim to be helpful to people?' he thought. 'Well, I'm going to try to do all the good I can – but I'm going to give myself a reminder never to lose my temper again.'

Thus Nathalan did a drastic thing. He locked a heavy chain around one of his ankles. This was painful and made it difficult for him to walk. Once the chain was in place he took the key of the lock to the top of a cliff and hurled it far out to sea. He would never see it again and the chain would be locked on his leg forever to remind him of his weakness.

Nathalan then set out on a pilgrimage to Rome. Trying to do good whenever he could, he reached the city absolutely tired out. Desperately hungry, he bought a fish in the market place. He went out into the countryside and built a little fire.

'I'm certainly ready for my supper,' he said to himself, as he cooked the fish on the fire. 'It looks as if it will be very tasty.'

The fish was soon ready and he started to slice it open with his sharp knife: almost at once the knife hit something sharp in the fish's body. Mystified, Nathalan prized it open carefully and . . .

He could hardly believe his eyes. There, lying inside the fish, was a key.

Nathalan closed his eyes and said a prayer. He knew, before even trying it, that it was the key which would unlock his chain.

He had been forgiven.

Information for the teacher

1 St Nathalan's feast day is on 8th January. If the 'food/crops' aspect of the story is developed, there are two other useful anniversaries: on the same date in 1940 food rationing was introduced in Britain; on 12th January 1948 Britain's first supermarket opened.

2 Some discussion could be generated about how forgiveness can be

shown, and children's experiences could be related here. A useful reference to supplement the discussion might include the King and the Governor (Matthew 18, 23–34).

3 Fish play an important role in the Bible: the disciples who were fishermen; the feeding of the five thousand (Matthew 14, 19–20); Jonah and the whale (Jonah 1, 1–17).

   The sign of the fish was used by early Christians as a secret sign. This was because the letters of the Greek word for 'fish' (pronounced 'icthus') are the first letters of the words meaning 'Jesus Christ, Son of God, Saviour'.

Hymn suggestion

Come and Praise Vol 1 'Water of life' No 2

Prayer

Let us pray this morning that we can control ourselves and not lose our tempers. In thinking about this, let us listen to the following words:

> Think of the body as a chariot
> Think of thoughts as the driver
> Think of the senses as the horses.
>
> He who has no understanding,
> Whose mind is not held firm,
> Whose senses are uncontrolled,
> Is like a vicious horse out of the control of its driver.
>
> He who has understanding,
> Whose mind is held firm,
> Whose senses are held under control,
> Is like a good horse in the hands of a firm driver.
>
> (Adapted from the *Katha Upanishad*.)

National Curriculum cross-curricular reference

English could be well served by the wide dramatic scope of this story. Science and Geography could be interwoven in considering areas such as aquatic life, fish as food, types of fish, where and how fish are caught. The location and significance of Rome could involve both Geography and History.

9 Here he comes

Introduction

Have you ever noticed how people are superstitious? They won't walk under ladders, they 'touch wood' or 'keep their fingers crossed'. This morning's story is about a woman who thought bad luck would come her way because of what a certain man had done . . .

Story

It was terribly hot in the city of Mecca. The air seemed to press down heavily and the dusty street was still and silent. A first man appeared, to be followed by another, and another. Women and children arrived too, and all crowded in small patches of shade. They made sure they could all see the street.

Soon a whisper went up. 'Here he comes.'

'Get ready!'

'She hasn't appeared yet.'

'Don't worry, she has never missed.'

Walking steadily along the street was a very calm-looking man. He looked neither to the left nor the right and was approaching a balcony which hung out over the street. As he neared the balcony a woman suddenly appeared on it. She had a bucket in her hands and moved purposefully to the edge of the balcony.

When the man was almost directly beneath her, with a scream, she hurled the contents of the bucket all over him. The thick dust and rubbish, sweepings from her house, dropped firmly on the man passing below.

'She never forgets,' said somebody among the watchers.

'Never. You know why she does it?'

'No. Tell me.'

'Well, that man is called Muhammad. Some people say he is a great prophet. He went to the mosque in the centre of town and threw out all the statues of gods. He says there is only one God.'

'But why did that bother the woman?'

'Ah well, lots of people think that if the gods are harmed a great disaster will befall Mecca and its people. This woman is just one of the people who want to get at Muhammad. He is very unpopular.'

The people went away; but exactly the same time the next day they were all there to see it happen again. Everybody knew when Muhammad went to pray and they knew the route he always took.

Then, one day, the woman was not there to throw down the rubbish. Nor was she there the next day, or the next.

Muhammad asked around. 'The woman who throws her rubbish down on me – where is she? I haven't seen her for three days.'

'Ah,' said one of the townspeople, 'she's ill, I think.'

So Muhammad went to the woman's house. After he had knocked for several minutes, a frail voice finally told him to come in.

'You're ill,' said Muhammad, looking at the woman as she lay pale and shaking on a chair. 'You must let me help you.'

The woman was too ill to say anything but she couldn't help wondering why this man whom she had treated so dreadfully had come to help her.

Muhammad cared for the sick woman – cleaning, cooking and making sure she had everything she needed. Slowly she recovered.

'Sir,' she said one day when she was feeling strong again, 'thank you for looking after me so well. Would you let me do something?'

'Of course,' replied Muhammad.

'May I come to the mosque with you and say a prayer too?'

So, by his actions, Muhammad had got the woman to believe his teaching.

Information for the teacher

1 To be considerate to others was one of Muhammad's basic teachings. Muslims consider the words of the Qur'an to be the words of God – as told to Muhammad by the angel Gabriel. There are many Muslim stories which emphasise caring for others.

2 Muhammad was born in Mecca (in about 570 AD Christian dates). Despite the presence of the famous shrine (the Ka'aba) in the city, Muhammad was concerned about its false gods. He and his followers suffered much abuse trying to establish that there was only one God.

He left to live in Medina but returned to Mecca in 630 when the city became fully Muslim, the idols were finally got rid of and the Ka'aba took on its great significance for the religion.

At least once in his or her lifetime every Muslim should take a pilgrimage (*hajj*) to Mecca.

3 A possible calendar link might be with other significant religious figures: Swami Vivekananda, the Hindu reformer, was born in 1862 on 12th January; Wilson Carlile who founded the Church Army was born in 1847 on the 14th.

Hymn suggestion

Come and Praise Vol 1 'Spirit of God' No 63

Prayer

In our prayer this morning, let us listen carefully to some words which were said by Muhammad. Let us then pause quietly for a minute to try and understand them.

'It is charity for any Muslim to plant a tree or cultivate land which provides food for a bird, animal or man.'

'Visit the sick, feed the hungry and free the captives.'

'Say part of your prayers at home so your houses do not become like graves.'

National Curriculum cross-curricular reference

Geography could be linked to a location of the Muslim world and in History some exploration of its growth and spread could be examined.

The story itself is a good one to dramatise and English could also be served by the sort of discussion it provokes.

10 Avalanche!

Introduction

January is a month when we often get snow. Snow can be beautiful and fun to play in – but it can also be dangerous. Sometimes in Alpine areas snow sweeps down mountainsides crushing and burying everything in its path. These rushes of snow are called 'avalanches'.

Story

'*Danger of avalanches. Those people in threatened areas are strongly advised to leave their houses.*'

The Swiss Radio broadcast this warning over and over again in the winter of 1947. Listeners took it very seriously and moved away from homes in dangerous areas, but Hans Altschwank was worried. As the village schoolmaster in Urteli, he knew that a party of boys were staying in a hut high above the village. They were skiing during the day and would not have heard the warning.

'Come on, Werner,' said Hans to his fifteen-year-old son. 'We'd better go up there and get those lads to safety.'

So father and son set off, and reached the hut just as the group of boys were getting ready to go skiing.

'I'm glad we've caught you,' said Hans, 'and I'm glad you're all dressed for skiing. We've got to get out of here – and quick!'

'Why, what's the problem?' asked one of the boys.

When Hans told them about the threatened avalanches several of the boys exchanged frightened looks, and all hurried to follow Hans and Werner down the mountain. But they didn't quite make it.

As they began their descent, they heard the sinister 'whooshing' noise of snow rushing down the mountainside behind them. It filled the group with terror.

'Dodge from side to side!' shouted Hans, and the skiers swerved desperately to miss the rushing snow. It seemed that they had made it – until suddenly the last boy was swept off his feet and, in seconds, was buried under the snow. 'I know where he is,' shouted Werner, and the group rushed back to where he was pointing now that the snow had swept past. Digging feverishly, they sighed with relief when a hand suddenly poked up through the snow – and wiggled its fingers.

'Hang on, we'll soon have you out,' shouted Werner. He grabbed the hand of the missing boy, whose name was Paolo. 'We'll soon . . .'

But no sooner had Werner started to shout again, when 'Whoosh!' . . . a second avalanche began its rush down the mountain, as fast as an express train. Once again the group scattered, except for Werner who steadfastly held onto Paolo's hand.

Now Werner was buried too, but the others scrambled back once the danger was past and began digging again. Gradually they freed the two bruised and frozen boys, and the party skied down to the village below.

The group of boys were given beds in barns, and Hans and Werner went back to their own home. They were exhausted and fell asleep as soon as they had eaten. But the danger was not over.

While the village was asleep, a third avalanche swept down the mountainside, crushing and burying the houses at its foot. Troops from a nearby army barracks were rushed in to help with the rescue and soon almost everybody was accounted for. Only three people were missing – Hans Altschwank, his wife, and Werner.

When the party of boys heard this they refused to leave. 'We've got to find them,' said their leader. 'Come on, let's get digging.'

The story had a happy ending. Werner was discovered safe and sound fairly quickly, and finally, after fifty-seven hours, Hans and his wife too were found safe and alive.

This was a story of friendship, help and determination, and it filled the newspapers of the world.

Information for the teacher

1 Some poetic licence has been used with this story. Werner was discovered fairly quickly and evacuated to another village along with the other boys. It was there that they heard of the Altschwank parents' rescue and they were so inspired by this that they journeyed to another buried village, Valgretto, and rescued a girl who had been given up for dead.
2 The boys in the story were from the Pestalozzi Children's Village at Trogen, in Switzerland. The Pestalozzi Villages were set up after the war to care for the thousands of children who had been left homeless, friendless, and without relatives after the fighting in Europe.

   Pestalozzi Villages still exist to teach skills to children from poorer countries so that they can return home and utilise their skills for the benefit of all.

   A useful address is: Pestalozzi Children's Village Trust, Sedlescombe, Battle, East Sussex, TN33 0RR.

Hymn suggestion

Come and Praise Vol 1 'He who would valiant be' No 44

Prayer

Let us give thanks this morning for those people whose quick thinking and determined courage save so many lives when disasters occur.

Let us learn from this example.

National Curriculum cross-curricular reference

Science and Geography would both be served by considering the causes of avalanches and the location of countries where they occur. In the context of this story features like fear, danger, hope and rescue could engender some good creative writing.

11 *It will be all right*

Introduction

Often, when we are tempted to do something we shouldn't, we try to make it easier for ourselves by saying, 'It will be all right.' This morning's story is a reminder about this saying.

Story

January is often a very cold, frosty, icy month. In Britain, in years gone by, it was often colder than it is now. The January of 1867 was absolutely freezing. Snow lay thickly on the streets of London, icicles hung from rooftops and windows and a brilliant blue sky covered the city.

On the 15th of the month crowds of people began to gather at Regent's Park. Snowball fights broke out and a few daring young men began to slide and skate on the ice of the lake.

'Look at them,' cried a young woman in the crowd, 'they're having fun – let's go and join them.'

'That's a good idea.'

'Great! Come on, hurry up.'

Not everyone was quite so enthusiastic and a few people muttered doubts.

'How do we know the ice is strong enough?'

'Aren't there too many on it already?'

'I'm sure it will crack.'

But the crowds of fun-seeking people ignored the doubters. 'It'll be all right,' they cried. 'The worst that can happen is you'll slip over and get your clothes wet!'

Crowds more piled on to the ice and the sounds of laughter echoed through the cold, crisp air. Then, above the laughter, a different sound was heard – a shrill cry of fear. Suddenly the air was filled with shrieks of panic and screaming. The ice had broken!

As wedges of ice broke and tipped their terrified occupants into the freezing water, there was a mad scramble to get to the safety of the banks. But as the crowd moved this way and that further platforms of ice cracked and broke. People who tried to pull friends out found themselves slipping into the water. Whole families crashed screaming through the ice.

Eventually the terrible scene calmed down. The lake, which had looked before like a glistening white sheet, was now a mass of broken ice platforms bobbing on the bitter water. Beneath the surface lay many of the skaters, drowned within minutes.

It hadn't been 'all right'.

Information for the teacher

1 Another of the severest winters recorded in Britain began on 13th January 1881. January was the month of mediaeval Frost Fairs which were held in many European cities. As well as the trading aspect of these there was entertainment such as bull and bear baiting. The latter obviously offers some further discussion material in an RE context.

2 Another possible development from this story is that disasters often throw up heroes or heroines. There are plenty of examples from the past but up-to-date newspaper cuttings will also soon build up into very useful modern source material.

3 The following poem was written by a nine-year-old girl. It captures the essence of the two sides of winter.

> Winter is a beautiful time of the year.
> But is it?
> Frost glistens.
> Ice sparkles dazzling white.
> This is the beauty of winter.
> But the beauty is just a covering,
> To a cold miserable world.
> Dark and dull,
> That starves the animals
> Who dare to come out in winter.

Hymn suggestion

Come and Praise Vol 2 'Lay my white cloak' No 112

Prayer

Let us think this morning about those words: 'It will be all right.' Let us pray that we might be given the wisdom, determination and strength of character to decide for ourselves whether something is 'all right' or not.

Let us pray that we may be given the strength to resist temptation, when we know deep down that what we are being tempted to do is wrong.

National Curriculum cross-curricular reference

There is great scope for Science here: cold weather – how does it come about? – what are the dangers of it? – how do we cope with it? The latter point could be extended into History in a Now and Then context. A geographical slant could consider where cold-weather places are.

This story could be the basis of some dramatic work in Art, and winter scenes in general are good possibilities here – sunsets, silhouettes of trees, 'Lowry'-type pictures of people at play in the snow, etc.

The 'temptation' angle could be unfolded in considerably more detail in an RE context.

12   The cut

Introduction

'Help!' You just never know when you might have to use this word, and you can only hope that somebody will be able to give you the help you need. Fortunately, there are many people who help us in different ways.

Story

Sue was nine. Her dad called her 'Speedy'.

'She never walks anywhere, that girl,' he was always saying, 'always runs – upstairs, downstairs, to school, back home again – run, run, run.'

One day Sue was running downstairs as usual. She didn't notice that Liz, her sister, had left a doll on the stairs. Sue tripped over it.

At the bottom of the stairs was a radiator. Sue hit the radiator head first. She felt a sharp, stabbing pain in her head. When she put her hand up to feel it, her hand came away covered in blood.

'Help, help!' cried Sue. 'I'm hurt.'

Mum, Dad, Liz and Paul all heard Sue's shout and rushed to the bottom of the stairs.

'Her head,' shouted Mum shakily. 'Look at the blood.'

Dad got his handkerchief out and held it tightly over Sue's head. Sue was trying to be brave – but she did not like the blood.

'Get the car out,' said Dad. 'She'll have to go to hospital.'

Mum rushed out with the car keys.

'Hospital,' thought Sue. 'I've never been to hospital before. I'm scared!' She looked at Paul and Liz, and she could see that they were scared too.

Soon the family were on the way to the hospital. Dad drove, and Paul and Liz squeezed in the front seat. Sue lay on the back seat with her head on Mum's knee. She had a clean cloth on her head now, but there was still a lot of blood.

Swinging in at the hospital gates, Dad called out, 'We'll have to follow that sign,' as he pointed to a sign saying Casualty.

As they entered the building, a nurse saw them coming. 'Follow me,' she said to Mum and Sue. Dad and the others stayed behind and Dad gave some details to another nurse.

Mum and Sue were shown into a small room where a doctor was washing his hands. 'Hmm,' he said, after looking at Sue's head. 'Nothing that a few stitches won't put right.'

'Stitches!' thought Sue. 'They'll hurt, for sure!'

Very carefully the doctor examined Sue's head. Then the nurse cut off some of Sue's hair and washed all round the large cut. Then she put some other stuff on and Sue thought it felt funny.

'Where's the machine?' she asked.

'What machine?' asked the nurse.

'You said you were going to do some stitching – don't you need a sewing machine for that?'

'Oh, you'll just have to put up with me doing it by hand,' smiled the doctor, who was already working very carefully on Sue's head. After a few minutes he finished what he was doing and came round and sat in front of her.

'You've been very brave, Sue,' he said. 'You might have a headache for a little while but you'll soon feel fit again.'

Dad, Paul and Liz were pleased to see Sue.

'Hi, Speedy,' said Dad.

Soon the family was back home.

'You've had a busy day,' said Mum.

'Yes,' said Sue, 'but I've learned a lot. Now I know exactly what happens when you hurt yourself.'

'That's when we need nurses and doctors and hospitals,' said Dad.

But Sue didn't hear him – she was already running upstairs!

Information for the teacher

1 A possible January calendar link for this story is with the 14th. On this date in 1875 one of the world's most famous doctors was born – Dr Albert Schweitzer.

2 Some useful addresses are as follows:

Royal Society for the Prevention of Accidents, Cannon House, The Priory, Queensway, Birmingham B4 6BS (bearing in mind this theme of an accident in the home);

Royal Association for Disability and Rehabilitation (RADAR), 25 Mortimer Street, London W1N 8AB;

Help the Aged, St James Walk, London EC1;

St John's Ambulance Brigade, 1 Grosvenor Crescent, London SW1X 7EE.

3 The theme could be extended to consider some people who have lived outstanding lives of giving service and help. One of the most famous is Mother Teresa.

Mother Teresa was born in Yugoslavia in 1910. Originally she went to India in 1948 to be a teacher but she was so shocked by the suffering and poverty that she decided her life's work must be to help those people in desperate need.

Her work has resulted in world fame and gifts of money and medicine from far and wide to help her mission. In 1979 she was awarded the Nobel Peace Prize.

Hymn suggestion

Come and Praise Vol 1 'When I need a neighbour' No 65

Prayer

This morning we are concentrating our thoughts on a particular word – Help.

Let us think very carefully about the following words of a Hindu saying: 'He who does not help to turn the wheels of this great world lives a lost life.'

National Curriculum cross-curricular reference

There is considerable scope for Science and Technology here – inventions, machines, developments which give help in a variety of ways. 'People who help' can extend the RE aspect, and this could be further developed and linked with Geography in examining wider world issues where help is required. History would be involved in tracing improvements over the years in things like medical care, diet, living conditions, hygiene, etc.

13 Be prepared

Introduction

Cubs, Brownies, Scouts and Guides all know how important it is to 'be prepared'. This morning's story is a reminder of the sort of thing that can happen when we are not prepared.

Story

'It's fantastic!'

'It'll be great, won't it?'

'Fancy us being chosen like this.'

The ten girls all crowded round each other. They were thrilled with the news. Cliff Crosby, the great singer, was coming back to his home village to get married and they had been chosen to form a 'passage of light' when he arrived.

To do this each of the girls had been given an oil lamp and when Cliff arrived photographers were to be there taking pictures of him going into the house with the girls' oil lamps lighting his way.

'We'd better get our lamps ready for when he comes,' said Julie. 'We'd better have them all lit so we are ready.'

'Will we have enough oil?' asked Sally.

'I've bought some spare oil,' said Mehnaz.

'So have I.'

'I haven't.'

As a result of their talking, the girls found that five of them had brought some spare oil for their lamps and five hadn't bothered.

'It doesn't matter,' said Jayna, one of the girls who hadn't brought any spare oil. 'He'll be here soon anyway.'

It was then that the telephone rang. It was Cliff's agent. 'There's going to be a delay, girls – but he'll be there some time this afternoon.'

Time began to drag and some of the girls fell asleep. They were awakened by the shrill ringing of the telephone. Sally answered it. At once the girls were awake and getting their oil lamps ready – but now there was a problem.

Because of the delay several of the lamps had gone out. Those girls who had brought extra oil to be prepared for such a happening quickly filled up their lamps and got them going again. The girls who hadn't brought spare oil panicked.

'Quick, lend me some of yours.'

'Oh come on, just a drop.'

'Why didn't we think to bring some spare?'

'Hurry, we'll have to go down to the shops and get some.'

So the five girls without oil dashed out of the house and headed for the shops. No sooner had they disappeared than a fleet of cars swept into the street.

Cliff and his agent got out of the first car, while newspaper reporters and TV cameramen jumped out of those behind.

'Right, let's get this romantic picture.'

'Cliff going into his old house . . .'

'. . . with the way being lit by some old oil lamps.'

Cliff's agent grinned at the girls. 'These pictures will be in newspapers all over the world,' he said. 'And think of the folks who'll see this on TV tonight.'

So the girls who were prepared were caught up in all the excitement – they must have been photographed forty times! When the other girls returned – the ones who hadn't bothered to bring any spare oil – the street was empty. They had missed everything.

Information for the teacher

1 This adaptation of the well-known Bible story of the Foolish Maidens could be used in conjunction with two others. The first is the story of the two men who built houses – the wise one on firm ground, the foolish one on sand.

These stories could then be contrasted with an example of how Jesus told his followers about the way they should listen carefully and heed what they had been told. The example could be of the Sower and the Seed.

The Bible references for all three stories are:

The Foolish Maidens: Matthew 25, 1–11

The Builders: Matthew 7, 24–27

The Sower and the Seed: Mark 4, 3–8

2 Two useful calendar references for this story are 17th January
  which is St Anthony's Day, and 5th January which is the birthdate
  of Robert Morrison in 1782.

Anthony lived between 250 and 350 years after the time of
Jesus. He became a hermit but such was his reputation for giving
wise advice that people travelled from great distances to seek it
from him.

Robert Morrison gave guidance in a different way. A missionary
to China, he risked his life to get copies of the Bible in Chinese
into the country.

Hymn suggestion

Come and Praise Vol 1 'The wise may bring the learning' No 64

Prayer

Christians believe that our lives can be guided by advice given in the
Bible.

Listen to the words of a Christian prayer:

> Lord of the loving heart,
> May mine be loving too;
> Lord of the gentle hands,
> May mine be gentle too;
> Lord of the willing feet,
> May mine be willing too;
> So may I grow more like to Thee,
> In all I say and do.
> Amen.

National Curriculum cross-curricular reference

This is another story which is very good for drama. English could be
further served by children relating their own experiences about when
they have been caught unprepared.

'Light' is a theme which has enormous scope for Science, with
plenty of opportunities for practical work. History could incorporate
an investigation of the development in street and house lighting over
the years.

14 A dog's life

Introduction

One of the saddest things about January is that many Christmas presents are abandoned in this month. Even sadder is the fact that many of them are dogs.

Story

If you like dogs and you visit Battersea Dogs' Home in London, then it is a good idea to walk quickly round its eighteen blocks and four hundred and fifty-six kennels. The reason for this is that, should you stop in front of one dog for any length of time, you will probably raise his hopes.

Remember that these dogs have been lost, given away, abandoned, deliberately hurt and thrown out, or have suffered all sorts of physical and mental cruelty. If they could talk, each one would have a harrowing tale to tell. Despite this they all want to be loved and be part of a good home, so if you stop and look too long . . .

As long ago as 1860 Charles Dickens was writing about the plight of ill-treated and abandoned dogs and in many ways things haven't changed much since his day. Battersea Dogs' Home takes in about eighteen thousand dogs during the course of any one year. The intake is particularly high after Christmas when dogs which have been given as pets suddenly find themselves abandoned by irresponsible owners who are not prepared to spend the time, effort and money necessary to look after a pet properly.

Some stray dogs have been deliberately taken away from their homes so that they cannot return; others are just shut out of their homes and left to wander around. There are also some dogs who become lost when they get separated from their owners.

Stray dogs wander around the streets on their own or in packs. From these problems, others grow. The dogs themselves are miserable, sometimes savage and are often suffering from some disease. They mess pavements, attack other animals and sometimes threaten people. It has been estimated that stray dogs are the cause of approximately two thousand road accidents each year, and the frightening thing is that there are almost half a million strays roaming our streets.

Battersea Dogs' Home and other similar organisations continue to fight the great difficulties these problems cause. Battersea Dogs'

Home is never closed to dogs and they can be given in there at any time of the day or night. Those which are genuinely lost are usually reunited with their owners; but for the strays, the wounded, and the neglected, care is taken to try to 'match' them successfully with new owners. First of all such dogs are nursed back to good health and then a careful note is taken of their temperament.

The work of the Battesea Dogs' Home never stops.

Information for the teacher

1 The Battersea Dogs' Home is in constant need of money to keep it running. If you would like to help this organisation, or others like it, the following addresses might be useful:

   The Dogs' Home, 4 Battersea Park Road, London SW8 4AA (Tel. 071 622 3626); The Secretary, National Canine Defence League, 1 Pratt Mews, London NW1 0AB (Tel. 071 388 0137); RSPCA, The Causeway, Horsham, West Sussex RH12 1HG (Tel. 0403 64181).

2 If it has been decided that something practical is to be done in connection with this assembly, the above addresses could be displayed around the school as reminders to any organised activity.

3 An ideal day to link with this material is the 17th, which is the feast day of St Anthony, the patron saint of all domestic animals. In some countries on this date such animals are still taken to church to be blessed.

4 According to local knowledge and experience the presence of one or two (well-behaved!) pets certainly adds to the atmosphere. Obviously parental help (bringing, displaying, looking after, taking away) is essential here.

Hymn suggestion

Come and Praise Vol 2 'All the animals' No 80
(Simon Fitter's hymn has become one of the most popular of hymns in schools. It is well worth committing this one to memory as it is so useful for so many occasions.)

Prayer

Let us pray this morning for pets everywhere – and, in particular, for dogs. Let us always remember what their needs are and treat them with care, affection and dignity. Amen.

National Curriculum cross-curricular reference

Science is an obvious link here – comparisons between animals and humans, needs, characteristics, longevity, health, body structure, etc.

For English, discussing and writing about animals provides a subject which most children are interested in.

15   *Peace and quiet*

Introduction

Doctors tell us that too much noise is bad for our health, but have you ever thought about what a noisy world we live in? This morning's story reminds us of this.

Story

Mr Robinson stood on the station platform. His day at work was over and he had a bit of a headache. He thought how glad he would be to get home.

'Look out! LOOK OUT!'

Suddenly, Mr Robinson realised that the man driving the parcel carrier along the platform was shouting at him.

'Oh, sorry,' he muttered, and stepped back. As he did so, he bumped into a young man carrying a radio.

'Oh, sorry,' muttered Mr Robinson again, but the young man didn't seem to hear. This wasn't surprising because his radio was turned up to full volume. The music coming out of it seemed all 'blurred round the edges', it was so loud.

When Mr Robinson finally got into the train it was very crowded. He had to stand between two ladies who had been shopping. They had to shout to make themselves heard.

'I'm ever so pleased I went up to the sales today.'

'Yes, there were some real bargains. Did you see . . .'

They talked like this all the way to where Mr Robinson got off the train.

'I'm glad of a bit of fresh air after that,' he thought as he set off to walk to his house. Unfortunately, there wasn't much fresh air about –

buses roared by, cars braked and accelerated and a particularly noisy motorbike boomed up the street.

'Home at last,' muttered the tired traveller as he turned into his garden gate, trying to ignore the noisy and smelly lawnmower which his next-door neighbour was using.

'Hello, dear,' called his wife as Mr Robinson unlocked the front door. 'Why don't you go straight upstairs and get changed? I just want to finish watching *Family Friends* on telly. Tea'll be ready soon.'

'All right,' replied Mr Robinson, who could hear the loud bangs of his son's video game coming from one of the bedrooms. As he wearily climbed the stairs his daughter burst out of her bedroom. 'Hi, Dad,' she called above the booming of her radio.

'Hi,' replied Mr Robinson, 'have you . . .'

It was no good. His daughter hadn't heard and she was now bounding downstairs.

Mr Robinson got to the bathroom and locked the door behind him. At that moment the dog which lived opposite started a bout of frenzied barking.

'Oh,' muttered Mr Robinson. 'Oh for a bit of peace and quiet.'

Information for the teacher

1 There are several follow-up possibilities linked to this theme – Why is noise bad for us? Are people considerate enough with regard to noise? What noises are necessary? What conditions are best for thinking?

2 One of the underlying themes of this story is of course consideration for others. Linking the two themes together could be helped by some quotations from religious sources:

'Be humble always and gentle. Be forbearing with one another and charitable.' (Ephesians 4, 2)

'Glory to God in the Highest, and on earth peace among men.' (Luke 2, 14)

'Men shall live in peace of mind on the open pastures.' (Ezekiel 34, 26)

'Anxiety brings premature old age.' (Ecclesiasticus 30, 24)

3 Many infant teachers will be familiar with the delightful book entitled *Peace and Quiet* by Jill Murphy. This pursues a similar theme and examines why Mr Bear can't sleep.

4 A useful calendar link for this assembly is with the week beginning 18th January. Every year this is designated as a time of quiet reflection and prayer for Christian Unity.

Hymn suggestion

Come and Praise Vol 2 'Spirit of peace' No 85

Prayer

Let us think this morning about the need for peace and quiet. It is something that everybody needs in life. Let us pray for those whose lives are affected by noise. Let us never be guilty of causing other people pain and discomfort through our thoughtlessness.

National Curriculum cross-curricular reference

There is a very obvious link with Science here! (AT2 level 3b: 'Know that human activity may produce changes in the environment that can affect plants and animals.')

There is also much scope for discussion and debate in English, as well as thoughtful practical activities in Technology.

16   Our daily bread

Introduction

I expect that all of us in assembly this morning had at least some bread yesterday. Bread is one of the commonest of the foods we eat. But what do we really know about it?

Story

We know that, about five thousand years ago, when the pyramids were being built, priests and officers in Egypt were paid part of their wages in loaves of bread. The Romans were so keen to make sure that people buying bread were not cheated that they set up bakeries in public places and had them carefully inspected and guarded.

The Greeks were so keen to keep bread free of germs that they made all bakers wear masks, and in Turkey any baker who failed to give proper value in his loaves was tortured.

The Great Fire of London in 1666 was supposed to have started in a baker's shop in Pudding Lane. As a result of this bakers were forbidden to use straw overnight on their oven fires so that the same thing would not happen again. When the 1800s were reached some bakers were thought to add alum to their loaves to make them whiter and therefore more tempting to customers. Two lines from the story of 'Jack and the Beanstalk' also had a very sinister meaning at this time:

> Be he alive or be he dead,
> I'll grind his bones to make my bread.

It was actually thought that one baker ground human bones to use as an ingredient in his bread.

In France, the great revolution which took place there in 1789 happened partly because although there was plenty of bread to buy people were so poor that they couldn't afford it.

So you see, when we get our sliced, pre-wrapped, hygienic loaf of bread from the supermarkets these days we are looking at something that has a very ancient and interesting history.

Information for the teacher

1 'Bread' has been a popular RE theme and the Bible abounds in references to it. In Bible lands it was an essential food and was made from wheat or barley ground with mortar and pestle.

  Bread features in such stories as the feeding of the five thousand (Mark 6, 31–46); it was always a popular gift and was often used in quotations – 'Man shall not live by bread alone' (Matthew 4, 4). The symbolism of bread reaches its highest point in the Holy Communion service.

2 One possible calendar link is that John Howard died on 20th January 1790. He was Sheriff of Bradford and it was mainly owing to his efforts that laws were passed to make sure that prisoners had adequate food and living conditions.

  Robert Burns was born on 25th January 1759. The poet's birthday is celebrated annually by Scots all over the world. No celebrations would be complete without the traditional eating of the haggis. A description of this – sheep's liver and heart, suet, oatmeal, served in the sheep's stomach and boiled for three hours – could contrast with the basic plain fare of bread.

Hymn suggestion

Come and Praise Vol 2 'Bread for the world' No 75

Prayer

Let us bow our heads and think about the words: 'Our Father, Give us this day our daily bread.'

Let us give thanks for the treasure of food.

Let us pray that those who haven't enough are given both hope and help. Amen.

National Curriculum cross-curricular reference

Science would allow for a closer study of bread – the conditions needed for the growth of its ingredients, how it is made and baked, its value in a healthy balanced diet, etc.

The history of bread could be researched more thoroughly. There are plenty of facts to discover which interest children (the torture inflicted on cheating Turkish bakers was that they were nailed to their bakery doors by their ears!).

This is a theme which would be enhanced by carefully chosen visits – ideal for January when options are obviously restricted.

17   Is it worth it?

Introduction

Think about your school building for a minute. How long has it been built? Can you imagine what the area was like before it was built? How long did it take to build? Who was involved in building it?

This morning's story is about a building – one of the world's most famous. The same sort of questions could be asked about it.

Story

If you went to your local travel agents you could probably get a brochure advertising a holiday in China. This might suggest a visit to the Great Wall of China because every year thousands of people walk short distances along it. You certainly couldn't walk along all of it in a short package holiday – it is 2,400 kilometres in length, and ten metres high. Two questions you might ask about this wall are Why was it built? and Was it worth it?

About two thousand years ago the Emperor Shih Huang Ti decided a wall was needed to keep enemies out of his country.

'Get it organised,' he said to his chief ministers.

'But your majesty,' they replied, 'who will want to work in such a hard and lonely place? How can we possibly get enough men to do the job?'

'Start by emptying the prisons. Get every prisoner we've got in the country and send him up to the north to work on the wall.'

'Yes, sir, but . . .'

'Move the army up there too. They can look after the prisoners and work on the wall as well.'

So began ten years of misery for thousands of people. Fearful that they might have to labour themselves, the overseers drove the workers with terrible cruelty. Hundreds of thousands laboured under severe weather conditions with the most primitive of tools and with practically nothing in the way of comfort when they weren't actually working. Not surprisingly, all sorts of diseases broke out and all were overworked in the rush to get the wall completed. Thousands of men died while working on the wall – but work never stopped. As a man died, his body was thrown into the rubble and the wall built on top of him.

There is an old legend which says that a man died for every stone in the Great Wall of China – you can imagine how many deaths this must have meant in 2,400 kilometres!

Information for the teacher

1 This assembly is obviously best suited for upper juniors and could provoke discussions on values, and an appreciation of how fortunate we are to live today when building can take place without such cruelty and loss of life.

'Building' is a theme which, in itself, can expand into a variety of RE considerations – foundations, co-operation, quality, purpose, etc. 'Barriers' is another useful theme.

2 A useful calendar connection with this story is the Chinese New Year. Located in late January or early February this goes through a cycle – for instance, 1994 is the year of the Dog, 1995 the year of the Pig, then subsequently Rat, Ox, Tiger, Rabbit, Dragon,

Snake, Horse, Sheep, Monkey, Rooster and then back to Dog again.

Chinese New Year is basically a family festival when houses are decorated and presents exchanged. Processions are held in the streets and '*Kung Hei Fat Choy*' is the New Year Greeting.

3 A useful Biblical link with this story is a comparison with the Tower of Babel. In this story God was displeased with His people and decided to teach them a lesson. They were in the process of building a huge tower when God caused all the workmen to suddenly start speaking different languages – as a result the project ended in confusion. (The word 'babel' has thus come to mean 'a scene of noise and confusion'.) Biblical reference: Genesis 11.

Hymn suggestion

Come and Praise Vol 2 'You can build a wall' No 91

Prayer

Let us think this morning of the many lessons people have learned through history. Let us give thanks for modern technology and a greater awareness of the needs of all people.

National Curriculum cross-curricular reference

Both History and Geography are obvious links here – particularly in dealing with the 'when and where' aspects of the Great Wall. Science and Technology could feature strongly in 'how' considerations, with scope for model-making. There is also considerable scope for work in Art here.

February

18 The recipe

Introduction

None of us likes people who are selfish. Listen carefully to this morning's story: it is about somebody who was selfish, and thought he was very clever.

Story

The king was hurt. As the king was the great lion, all the other animals were very concerned. The hare went to see him.

'My lord,' said the hare. 'That was a great battle you won, but you have been badly hurt. You must rest until your wounds have fully healed.'

'Rest? Rest?' snarled the lion. 'I must eat, mustn't I?'

'Don't worry about that,' replied the hare. 'All the other animals want their king to recover. They will help, and I will prepare good meals and look after you.'

The lion hesitated. He was more badly hurt than he had at first realised. It would be good to be looked after and rest until he was well again. But could he trust the hare? He would see.

'Very well,' he replied firmly. 'You may be my servant, Hare.'

So the long healing process began. The hare was as good as his word. He made the lion comfortable, got his meals ready, arranged the times for visitors. He was an excellent servant, but the lion was very slow in getting completely better.

As time went by, the hyena grew to envy the hare more and more. 'What a job he's got,' he thought. 'Everything provided for him and safe as houses in the home of the king. He must be the luckiest animal alive at the moment. I'd like his job, and I've got a pretty good idea of how to get it.'

So the hyena made an appointment to see the lion. The hare

arranged it, greeted the hyena pleasantly, and then left him alone with the lion.

The hyena bowed low before the lion.

'My lord,' said the hyena, 'the animals are all very worried that you are not better by now.'

The lion gave a growl that could have meant anything.

'So they have sent me to be their spokesman,' went on the hyena. 'They don't think the hare is looking after you properly. They think I could do a better job – especially as there is a recipe for a meal which I'm sure would make you feel much better. That hare is just too lazy to make it.'

Now while the hyena was saying this, the hare, who was just about to come into the room, heard everything. He stepped inside quickly and spoke at once to both the lion and the hyena.

'No, no,' he said. 'You're quite wrong there, friend Hyena. I've got everything ready for that special meal – I was only waiting until I could get the last ingredient which, as I'm sure you know, is hyena flesh.'

As the hyena listened to what the quick-witted hare was saying, a chill of fear ran through him.

The lion gave a snarl, and bared his huge teeth. Without another word, the hyena leapt up and fled as fast as he could.

(Adapted from an old African folk tale.)

Information for the teacher

1 With a plot typical of so many folk tales this is the type of story young children enjoy. Folk tale anthologies regularly appear and a useful source for reviews and information is the children's book magazine, *Books for Keeps*, published at 6 Brightfield Road, Lee, London SE12 8QF.

2 A very useful date and story to link with this one are 1st February 1811 and the tale of Bell Rock Lighthouse. On 1st February 1811 the lighthouse was opened which warned shipping off the dangerous Inchcape Rock.

   In earlier years a bell had been put on this rock to warn ships but a pirate named Ralph the Rover, in a mood of bravado, cut away the bell and it sank. Later on, returning from a voyage, his own ship hit this rock and sank, taking the pirate leader down with it.

Hymn suggestion

Come and Praise Vol 2 'You can build a wall' No 91

Prayer

Dear God,
Help us to avoid the sin of selfishness, and teach us to be aware that trying to trick people in order to gain things for ourselves often leads to unhappiness.

Help us to learn how to be content, thoughtful and modest. Amen.

National Curriculum cross-curricular reference

The world of folk tales, similar stories and themes which transcend ethnic origin is a useful area for discussion in English. Such stories have the added bonus of often being ideally suited for drama.

19 What's inside?

Introduction

You will certainly know the person standing next to you in assembly this morning. But if you didn't, and you looked carefully at him or her, you would see face, eyes, hair, clothes – but you wouldn't know what he or she was like 'inside'.

Story

If you go to London and walk along by the river on the Thames Embankment you come to a rather strange monument. It is made of weather-beaten stone and points towards the sky like a long stone finger. This is Cleopatra's Needle, and it has an interesting history.

Cleopatra was an Egyptian Queen who lived hundreds of years ago and this monument once stood in Egypt. When it was decided that it should be brought to England it was found that inside it someone had put lots of souvenirs of the time when it was built. Things like children's dolls and ladies' jewellery were discovered.

The monument was then brought on a long, adventurous journey by sea to England. When it arrived there was a lot of discussion by the experts who had to decide what to do with it.

'We must put it up in an important position.'

'We want as many people as possible to see it.'

'What about putting something inside it too?'

'How do you mean?'

'Well, if it's ever moved, or opened up again, the people who move it will be able to see the sort of things we use today in our time.'

'What a good idea.'

It was decided to put the monument up beside the River Thames where it now stands. Inside it were put some children's toys, a few mirrors, a telephone directory, a number of newspapers, some photographs of ladies of the day showing fashions, and a packet of razor blades.

So, when you are in London, try and go to see Cleopatra's Needle and as you look at it think of the treasures which are inside it.

In a way it's a bit like people – what we look at and see certainly doesn't tell us about the treasures that lie inside.

Information for the teacher

1 Cleopatra lived from 69 to 30 BC. The obelisk which is Cleopatra's Needle stands 68 feet high and once stood at Heliopolis. It was during the last century that it was brought to England and therefore its inner contents already reflect another bygone era.

2 This theme of 'what lies within' is very evocatively told in the story of Caedmon. Caedmon, a poor cowherd, was at a farmhouse party. The guests sat in a circle and a harp was passed from one to another. Each guest sang and played when the harp reached him.

Caedmon had a terrible voice so before the harp reached him he slipped off and went to bed. He dreamed that a stranger came and told him 'to sing God's praises'. Knowing he couldn't sing, Caedmon was mystified. He sought advice at the great monastery at Whitby. There it was found that after reading passages from the Bible he could immediately rephrase them into wonderful poetry.

So Caedmon began to 'sing God's praises' and spent the rest of his life in the monastery rewriting sections of the Bible in language people could understand and enjoy.

3 For those in a position to do so, a visit to see Cleopatra's Needle would be an excellent follow-up to this story. February would be a good month for such an urban visit.

Hymn suggestion

There is something to be said for using two hymns in this assembly. This would depend on how the presenter has developed the theme, but the two suggestions are:
Come and Praise Vol 2 'In the bustle of the city' No 101
Come and Praise Vol 1 'Song of Caedmon' No 13

Prayer

Dear God,
Let us think this morning about what makes us ugly: telling lies, being rude, acting in a jealous, selfish, cruel or thoughtless way.
   Let us think about what makes us beautiful: always being ready with a kind word, thinking the best of people, caring about the thoughts and feelings of others.
   Help us to be beautiful, and not ugly, people. Amen.

National Curriculum cross-curricular reference

There is great scope for further historical and geographical development and research in a more detailed examination of the full story of Cleopatra's Needle.
   Science and Technology could be actively and practically involved in considerations of 'how monuments are erected – stand straight – remain in place'.
   There is plenty of related work in English too. Both discussion and written work might be embraced in considering what modern artefacts we would choose to lodge in a monument today; what the most desirable inner qualities of human beings are, etc.

20 Judy

Introduction

This morning's story is about a boy called Evan Davies. One thing you could certainly say about him is that he didn't give up easily.

Story

'Great, great, just what I wanted.'
   Evan's eyes lit up with delight when he saw what his eleventh birthday present was. The 'present' looked pretty happy too – she

was a mischievous Jack Russell puppy whom Evan promptly christened Judy.

Evan's birthday was in February and in the months that followed he and Judy became almost inseparable companions. When the summer holidays arrived, Evan looked forward to having even more time to spend with his pet.

'We're going to go on the longest walks ever,' said Evan to Judy, playfully tickling one of her ears. Judy wagged her tail fiercely.

Next morning the two of them were up early and off exploring the countryside round their home in Builth Wells, Mid Glamorgan.

'Judy . . . Judy . . . come on,' called Evan, when he realised it was time to get back home for dinner. Instead of the normal excited barking there was silence.

'Judy . . . Judy!'

This time a note of alarm crept into Evan's voice. Running back to where he had last seen Judy, Evan called out her name again and again. He whistled and shouted but there was no reply. Finally, with tears streaming down his face, Evan ran home.

'Well, it doesn't sound too good, I'm afraid,' said his mother when he told her. 'You know there are a lot of rabbit holes up there. Judy must have crawled into one, got stuck and couldn't get out. We'll go and have a look, but don't build your hopes up.'

So mother and son followed the path of the last walk, whistling and shouting and looking everywhere where the little dog might be trapped. Mrs Davies looked at the many rabbit holes, and felt that, sadly, they would never see Judy again.

'I know she is still alive somewhere,' said Evan, after the fruitless search. 'I just know it.'

So began a lonely routine for Evan. Every morning and evening he followed the now familiar path to where Judy had disappeared. Once he reached the area of the rabbit holes he called her name for about five minutes, then made his weary way home.

Mrs Davies looked on with concern, but admired her son's determination. One week went by, then another. Day after day Evan went and returned, went and returned, his face set firmly.

Then, thirty-six days after Judy's disappearance, Evan and a friend were out calling when suddenly . . .

'I heard something.'

'You sure?'

'Definitely.'

'Well . . .'

'Listen, there it is again.'

'It's . . . it's . . . it's a bark! Faint, but definitely a bark.'

Events then moved quickly. On hearing the news, neighbours with spades rushed to the spot where the faint barking was heard and began digging. As they dug, the barking, although desperately weak, seemed to get nearer.

Finally the rescuers broke through a warren of rabbit holes and there was the long lost dog. Almost dead through lack of food and water, Judy was in a desperate condition – but it was nothing that love and care could not put right. And with Evan as a master it was certain she would get as much of that as she needed!

Information for the teacher

1 The happy conclusion to this story occurred in September 1990 but it is included here because Judy was a February birthday present. This in itself might be a useful starting point after ascertaining which children have birthdays – and what their presents were.
2 Animal – and particularly dog – stories are always popular with children. Useful sources for more material are: *The Guinness Book of Pet Records*, ed. G L Wood (Guinness); the RSPCA, The Causeway, Horsham, West Sussex RH12 1HG; the Battersea Dogs' Home, 4 Battersea Park Road, London SW8 4AA.
3 A useful comparison with this story, in this case a dog's devotion to its owner, is the story of Greyfriars Bobby. Bobby was a Skye terrier so devoted to his master that when the latter died the little dog 'guarded' his grave for fourteen years. In doing so he became one of the most famous and best-loved dogs in Edinburgh – and his fame ultimately spread much further. Note: *Greyfriars Bobby* by Lavinia Derwent (Puffin).

Hymn suggestion

Come and Praise Vol 1 'Lost and found' No 57

Prayer

Let us bow our heads and think quietly about the message of this morning's story. Many people and creatures would not have survived without other people's determination to try and help as long as necessary. Let us pray that we might be given this kind of determination and dedication.

National Curriculum cross-curricular reference

Areas which could be investigated in Science: what we, and animals, need for survival; durability in extremes; survival techniques, etc.

'Requirements for turning in a tunnelled area' is a theme which could be pursued in Technology.

21 This month

Introduction

February is always the shortest month of the year but there are many interesting things about it – both indoors and outside.

This month

Many people think one of the best things about February is that flowers start appearing after the long winter. These include the small white flowers which are called snowdrops. They are a sign of hope for the spring which is now a little nearer, but they are also called the 'flowers of hope' for another reason. An old story is that when Adam and Eve were sent out of the Garden of Eden an angel turned a snowflake into this flower to give them some hope for the future. Crocus buds can also be seen pushing up during this month.

It is worth keeping an eye on trees in February. The hazel starts to have a furry appearance because of its catkins and high up in tall trees there is a lot of activity going on. Rooks in particular are busy getting their nests ready. Sometimes they do this by repairing old ones and sometimes they pull the old ones to pieces and start again on new ones. The sounds of birds singing can begin during February and most probably it will be the voices of blackbirds or thrushes which you hear.

Indoors in February, the 2nd is a special day. This was the day on which Mary took the baby Jesus to be blessed at the temple. To remember this candles are lit in churches and blessed for the whole year. This date is known as Candlemas.

Pancake Day is one all children enjoy. It came into being because people once used up all their eggs and fat on this day. This was because it was just before a time called Lent – when people did without certain foods for forty days to remind themselves of Jesus's life.

All Scouts, Guides, Brownies and Cubs will know that 22nd February is a special time for them, called Thinking Day.

Finally, if at any time during this month you are having beans for lunch, have a closer look at them. They probably don't look very special but if you were Japanese you could enjoy having them this month. This is because in February Japanese people throw beans at each other – this is supposed to send winter away!

Information for the teacher

1 Carrying beans as protection against demons and witches is a long-held folk tradition in many cultures. A man with a bean ready in his mouth was considered to be well prepared if he met a witch – he simply spat the bean at her.

2 In the time when Jesus was born it was the custom of every Jewish mother to take her first male child to the temple forty days after he was born. The child was then presented to the Lord and the mother was blessed. Candlemas is therefore the fortieth day after Christmas.

3 Pancake Day – Shrove Tuesday – is the forty-first day before Easter and the day before Ash Wednesday, which begins Lent. In days when there was more revelry and feasting before Lent the day before Shrove Tuesday was known as Collop Monday – when large pieces of fried meat were eaten.

Hymn suggestion

Come and Praise Vol 1 'At the name of Jesus' No 58

Prayer

Let us give thanks this morning for time. Let us learn to enjoy each month and know about it as it comes round during the year.

Let us make the most of every minute, hour, day, week and month of our lives.

National Curriculum cross-curricular reference

Both History and Geography can be involved in any 'time' work. History could be linked to relevant events; Geography to 'how it works'. Science can be incorporated too, in connection with this latter point, and also in its relationship to the natural world.

As with all months there are artistic possibilities in February – careful observation and painting of snowdrops might be one of them.

22 Patience

Introduction

One of the qualities we need in our lives is patience. We just can't get exactly *what* we want exactly *when* we want it – as this story reminds us.

Story

'I'm so hungry,' thought the crow as he flew along. 'What I wouldn't give for a . . . what's that?'

Out of the corner of his eye he had seen a rich, ripe mango hanging on a tree. Swooping down, he perched on a branch beside the mango.

'You're just what I've been looking for,' said the crow. 'I'm going to enjoy eating you so much.'

'Well, that's fine,' answered the mango. 'I'm ripe and I should be eaten. Before you eat me, though, you must wash your beak!'

The crow agreed to do this but could find no pot to get water from the well. Hurrying to a potter he asked the man to make him a pot.

'Certainly, certainly,' said the potter, 'if you bring me some clay.'

When the crow got to a field to get some clay the field told him that he needed to find a deer with a strong horn to dig up the clay. Getting very hot and flustered, the crow flew off and found a deer.

'Certainly, certainly,' answered the deer in reply to the crow's question. 'But first I will need some milk from a cow.'

The crow flew off again and soon found a cow. He explained to the cow what he needed and the cow said: 'Certainly, certainly, but before I can give you any milk I'll have to have some grass to eat.'

Back to the field flew the crow.

'Now I want some grass before I want some clay,' he gasped. 'Let me have some grass please, Field.'

'Aaah,' said the field, 'you can certainly have some grass – but you'll need a sickle to cut it with.'

Once again the crow flew off. This time he went to a blacksmith and explained what he needed.

'Certainly, certainly,' said the blacksmith. 'I'll give you a sickle but I'll have to sharpen it first or else it won't cut the grass.'

So the blacksmith put the sickle into a hot fire and sharpened it.

'Quickly, quickly,' said the crow, thinking of the beautiful mango.

'But it's too hot to carry yet,' said the blacksmith. 'You must wait until it cools down.'

'Nonsense,' said the crow, 'I haven't time for that. Put it on my back and let me be off.'

So the blacksmith put the sickle on the crow's back. Immediately there was a terrible smell of burning feathers and the crow, in great pain, found that now he couldn't even fly.

Meanwhile, back at the tree, the mango waited and waited and waited for the crow with the clean beak to come and eat. Finally it became so ripe that it could hang onto the tree no longer and it fell to the ground.

(Adapted from an Indian 'village story')

Information for the teacher

1 *Indian Village Stories* by P Mohanti (Davis-Poynter) is an excellent source for stories like this.
2 A useful February link for this story is the Hindu festival of Sarasvati Puja. Sarasvati is the Hindu goddess of learning, wisdom and knowledge. She would be the source of sound advice about life, and about foolish attitudes such as are portrayed in this story.

Hymn suggestion

Come and Praise Vol 2 'Time is a thing' No 104

Prayer

Let us bow our heads and think of patience.
Patience to bear with disappointment,
Patience to bear with hardship,
Patience to bear with dangers.
Lord, give us the strength to have this quality.

(Very loose adaptation from the Qur'an)

National Curriculum cross-curricular reference

'The Indian village' could provoke a lot of research and investigation in Geography. This could spill over into Science when considering weather, difficulties, etc, and the latter might then provoke some thoughts in Technology.

23 Pass it on

Introduction

Have you ever thought about how the way you behave affects other people? This morning's story might act as a reminder.

Story

It was a cold February Monday morning and Jason got out of bed feeling really down in the dumps. He'd been moved in class to sit next to the new kid; he was sure he wouldn't be in the football team after Friday night's practice; and it seemed they were going to have that miserable supply teacher again.

By the time he'd lost a button off his shirt and found that Julie had been using his toothbrush, he was even more tetchy.

'Come on, Jason, hurry up or you'll be late.'

'Hmm.'

'Come on, eat your breakfast.'

'Leave off, Mum.'

On his way to school Jason passed a line of shop windows. The shops weren't open yet and as he looked at his reflection one of the most miserable faces he'd ever seen stared back at him. Window after window showed the same unhappy face until, as the last window came up, Jason spread his mouth wide and the reflection came to life with his smile. A woman was passing in the opposite direction and as soon as Jason smiled, she not only smiled back but she bade him a cheerful 'Good Morning'.

Immediately he felt better. Some of the gloom seemed to lift, and the first person he bumped into in the playground was the new kid – who looked nervous.

Seeing Jason's smile the new kid came up to him. 'Jason . . . I just wanted to say . . . I'm glad Wattie moved you to sit beside me . . . I'm really glad.'

Jason slapped the new kid on the back and they moved into line together as the whistle went. Mr Clarke, the teacher in charge of games, was on duty and as the classes filed in he took Jason by the arm.

'Football,' he said. 'You don't need me to tell you that you didn't play well in Friday's practice. So Alex is going to be in the team for the next match . . . but keep trying – your turn is sure to come again.'

When Jason smiled and nodded his head Mr Clarke slapped him on the back.

'I knew you would take it like the real sportsman you are. Well done.'

In a funny sort of way, Jason felt as if he'd scored the winning goal rather than been dropped from the team.

After assembly the class bustled into their room as usual. They already knew Wattie was away on a course and when the supply teacher came in the first person she looked at was Jason.

Jason smiled, and said, 'Good morning, Miss.'

The supply teacher nodded, and then said, 'I've got some really interesting old newspapers for you to look at this morning.'

And they *were* interesting too! In fact the whole day seemed to go with a real swing.

That afternoon, as Jason walked home, he paused at the shop windows again.

'Funny', he thought, 'that smile seemed to make all the difference.'

Information for the teacher

1 In pursuing the idea of the value of a smile, these are some relevant February anniversaries: P G Wodehouse, creator of Bertie Wooster and Jeeves, died on 14th February 1975; David Garrick, one of England's greatest actors who played many roles in comedy, was born on 19th February 1717; Baron Münchhausen, teller of fantastic and amusing tales, died on 22nd February 1797; Stan Laurel, of Laurel and Hardy fame, died on 23rd February 1965.

2 A little poetic licence could be used with the following quotation: 'Every day, and in every way, I am becoming better and better.' Originally designed as an auto-suggestion catch-phrase by the

French psychotherapist Emile Coué, it could be linked to this assembly story and ensuing work.

Another useful phrase in this context is one coined by Sir Wilfred Grenfell: 'It's not what you have that matters. It's what you do with what you have.'

Hymn suggestion

Come and Praise Vol 2 'You shall go out with joy' No 98

Prayer

Dear God,
Help us to be the sort of person other people are pleased to meet. May we smile more than we frown; may we encourage more than we criticise; may we look for good points rather than bad points. Amen.

National Curriculum cross-curricular reference

English, particularly via drama, is an obvious link here. An examination of how muscles work (as, for instance, in changing our facial expressions) would bring in some Science activity. There is also some scope for Music in the context of 'sounds which make us smile . . . feel good . . .', etc.

24 Rescue

Introduction

If you ever desperately need help then you should hope that it would come from a man like Patrick Sliney. This is his story.

Story

February 10th, 1936, brought with it some of the worst weather anybody could remember in the fishing village of Ballycotton in Ireland. Howling gales tore slates off roofs, people were blown over in the streets, and rocks were torn from the harbour wall.

It was in these conditions that Patrick Sliney, coxswain of the Ballycotton lifeboat, heard that the Daunt Rock lightship had broken loose from its moorings. It was now adrift in the tumultuous seas and the only hope for the eight men on board was – the Ballycotton lifeboat.

Patrick and the seven crew members boarded their boat and set out into the terrifying seas. By noon they had spotted the drifting lightship.

'We've got to get a wire hauser across to her and then we'll pull her into shore,' said Patrick.

For hours the seamen tried to get the two ships tied together. Every time they got the wire rope fixed, a terrible wave crashed the ships apart and the rope snapped. After twenty-four hours the lifeboat had to give up the attempt and put into the nearest port to refuel. None of the men on board had had any food during this time.

Snatching a quick rest and some food while their boat was being refuelled, the men gazed anxiously at the weather, hoping it might improve. It got worse.

Putting to sea again, the lifeboat tried again to get a tow rope on the lightship. When this failed Patrick decided more drastic action had to be taken.

'She's drifting towards Daunt Rock,' he told the lifeboat crew. 'If she hits that, all aboard are done for.'

'What can we do, Skip?' asked one of the crew.

'Well, the only way to get those lads off,' replied Patrick, 'is to get our boat close enough for them to jump.'

'But if they miss they'll be doomed for sure.'

Patrick's look told the seaman he already knew this. He gave orders for the lifeboat to be steered as near as possible to the bucking, rearing lightship.

On the first run there was enough time for only one man to jump safely aboard before the waves pushed the two boats apart. Time after time Patrick steered the lifeboat alongside with great skill. One by one the men managed to jump off the lightship until the lifeboat became damaged by the sea hurling the two ships together.

'There's only two of them left,' shouted one of the crew, above the shrieking gale.

'Yes, but look at them,' cried Patrick.

The two men left on the lightship were hanging outside the guard rail. They had climbed there ready to jump but were so exhausted they had no strength to climb back.

'They're too done for even to jump,' shouted Patrick. 'We'll have to get so close this time that they can be snatched off the side. Any volunteers to do the snatching?'

Every man on the crew volunteered and Patrick edged the lifeboat nearer once again. The waves pounded the ships and the gale tore frantically at the drenched and exhausted men. Nearer . . . nearer . . . nearer . . .

Finally, close enough to snatch the dangling men, the lifeboat crew seized them and dragged them to safety. Thankfully, Patrick turned the boat for home. Seventy-six hours after they had set out, he and the crew of the Ballycotton lifeboat had completed their task and eight men's lives had been saved.

Information for the teacher

Ballycotton is situated on the southern coast of Eire and is one of the 134 offshore lifeboat stations of the RNLI. This organisation was founded in 1824. Its address is: Royal National Lifeboat Institution, West Quay Road, Poole, Dorset D15 1HZ.

Hymn suggestion

Come and Praise Vol 1 'He who would valiant be' No 44

Prayer

Let us bow our heads and pray this morning for those men and women who work on ships of all shapes and sizes.

Let us pray that they may be kept safe in storms and dangerous weather.

Let us pray particularly for the crews of lifeboats whose work is to try to save others, often in very dangerous conditions.

National Curriculum cross-curricular reference

The development of life-saving at sea is a very far-reaching History theme. The locating of some of the coastal lifeboat stations would be a fruitful task in Geography, and both Science and Technology could be involved in considering ships and how and why they float. In Music, the sea offers many compositions to listen to and talk about, ranging from the overture to Wagner's *The Flying Dutchman* to Debussy's *La Mer*.

25 We need a king!

Introduction

Sometimes, we complain about certain things in our lives: 'I wish I could stay up later to watch TV . . . I wish I didn't have to go outside on cold playtimes . . . I wish my brother didn't sleep in the same room as me' . . . and so on.

This morning's story will give those who complain something to think about.

Story

'We need a king! . . . We need a king! . . . We need a king!' The frog chorus croaked over the ponds and lakes. They had had a long meeting and decided that they were as important as anyone else, so . . .

'We need a king . . . we need a king!'

High above, the gods heard the croaking.

'What's all that about?'

'It's those frogs – they want a king.'

'But why? They've always lived peacefully together until now.'

'You know how it is – somebody starts to complain and before you know where you are . . .'

'I know – "We need a king".'

The gods thought about how helpful the frogs had previously been to each other, and how peaceful they had been. Perhaps this problem could be solved easily. So, one of the god's messengers arranged for a big log to be thrown into the lake.

'Your king has arrived,' he called, as the log hit the lake with an enormous splash.

The frogs were impressed. Their new king was very big. He didn't say a lot but he looked very powerful.

For a few days the frogs kept away from the king, until two of them swam close, and dared each other to jump on his back. One frog took a deep breath and leaped up onto the log.

When nothing happened other frogs jumped on the log too. Soon they were calling out again.

'Our king's useless.'

'He can't even move.'

'He's not a proper king at all.'

'We need a king . . . we need a king . . . we need a king!'

Once again the gods heard the cry and this time they decided the frogs needed a proper lesson.

Later that day a stork flew to the edge of the large lake and called out.

'Frogs – I am your new king, and I want to see my subjects. Show yourselves.'

'That's better,' thought the frogs. 'A proper king who gives orders and looks important.'

So from every bit of rock and mud and water the frogs came out to acknowledge their king.

No sooner did he see them than the stork swept forward and began eating frogs as fast as his huge beak could cram them in.

The frogs were terrified. They dodged away to safety, shivering with fear.

'Oh – if only we had been satisfied,' said one of them.

Information for the teacher

1 This well-known fable has virtually limitless possibilities for adaptation and improvisation. It is the sort of material which can also be very simply dramatised for assembly purposes.
2 A possible calendar link for this story is 12th February, when Charles Darwin, the naturalist, was born.
3 This story, with its mixture of foolishness and wisdom, could be linked very appropriately to an anonymous verse which emphasises the same qualities via a 'creature' source:

> The wise old owl sat high in an oak,
> And the more he heard the less he spoke,
> The less he spoke the more he heard,
> So why can't we be like that wise old bird?

Hymn suggestion

Come and Praise Vol 1 'He's got the whole world' No 19

Prayer

Dear God,
Help us to remember that no life is perfect and that we will all suffer disappointments. Teach us to value the good things in our lives and help us to try and show how much we appreciate these. Amen.

National Curriculum cross-curricular reference

English would be very well served here by using this story as a basis
for discussions, and then as a starting point for creative writing linked
to its theme. There seem to be strong possibilities for Art, and even
Music. In the latter some improvisation could be linked to the
differing 'moods' of the story.

26   Two's company

Introduction

Have you ever known anyone whom you really liked – but you
couldn't understand why they behaved badly? If so, this morning's
story will make you think.

Story

In all of Italy there was no more beautiful girl than Katharine. Sad to
say, few people were as rude or as bad tempered either!

Petruchio was a lively and clever young man, and when he arrived
in the town where Katharine lived, he soon heard of her reputation.

'I wonder why she behaves like that?' he thought. 'And I wonder if
I can get her to change her ways?'

He went to visit her.

'Get out of here, you stupid oaf,' shouted Katharine when
Petruchio called on her. 'Out – right now.'

'How kind of you to ask me to stay,' replied Petruchio. 'You are
most generous.'

'Are you mad?' screeched Katharine. 'Are you deaf? I *don't* want
you to stay. I want you to get out – NOW!'

'Please, please,' interrupted Petruchio. 'I don't really need any
persuading to stay. Thank you again.'

Katharine was mystified. Every time she met this strange man
again she hurled insults at him – and he treated them as if they were
compliments!

Wherever she turned, Katharine seemed to bump into Petruchio.
Meanwhile, he had come to like her very much. One day he
staggered her by asking her to marry him.

'*Marry* you? Marry *you*?' screamed Katharine. 'Never. I'd sooner
see you hanged than marry you.'

'Thank you, my dear!' exclaimed Petruchio. 'I'm so glad you've said yes. You've no idea how happy that makes me.'

Then, to the astonishment of Katharine, he told her that he had made all the arrangements for their wedding.

The day of the wedding soon arrived. Katharine, working herself up into one of her worst tempers, prepared to give Petruchio the worst possible time. Marry him, indeed!

But when Petruchio arrived Katharine got another shock. Instead of the neat, charming man she had got to know, Petruchio turned up dressed like a beggar and began to shout and insult everybody there except Katharine. She was so astonished and surprised by his behaviour that, before she knew what was happening, she was married and on the way home with her husband!

'You – get that door open quickly,' shouted Petruchio to a servant when they arrived. 'I hope my wife's food is ready – now get out!'

Petruchio led the dazed Katharine into a large dining room where a most beautiful feast was laid out. Despite her confused feelings Katharine suddenly realised she was absolutely starving. She moved hungrily towards the table.

'No!' shouted Petruchio. 'No, my sweet, that food is nothing like good enough for you. Servants, take it away!'

Before Katharine could take a bit the feast was removed. By now, exhausted, confused and speechless, she wanted nothing more than to go to bed. Telling her husband this she sank gratefully into a large and comfortable bed – only to find that within seconds Petruchio was beside the bed, hurling off the covers.

'No, no. You can't sleep here. This bed is nothing like good enough for you. Servants, you idle lot, take this bed away at once.'

This went on for days, until the couple paid a visit to Katharine's father's home. He was amazed to find his daughter quiet, polite and helpful!

For a day or two more, Petruchio played the part of the noisy bully. Then, seeing that Katharine was cured of her bad-tempered, rude ways, he became his charming, considerate self again. From that point on the pair were one of the happiest couples in the whole of Italy.

Information for the teacher

1 Teachers will recognise the characters and plot of Shakespeare's *The Taming of the Shrew*, or, in more modern Hollywood guise, *Kiss me, Kate*.

This seems an ideal story to use on St Valentine's Day, 14th February, with all its connotations.

2 The opportunity should not be lost to discuss something of the origins of St Valentine's Day. There were in fact two Valentines, both Italians: one a bishop and one a priest. Both were executed for refusing to give up their Christian faith but it is the priest, who was also a physician, around whom the most famous legend grew up.

Valentine, knowing full well that Christians should be handed over to the Romans, chose instead to hide them from their persecutors. He also broke a Roman law by marrying couples although marriage was forbidden. He was caught and sent to prison to await execution. There he befriended one of the guards and restored the sight of his blind daughter. He was beheaded on 14th February 269.

Hymn suggestion

Come and Praise Vol 1 'A man for all the people' No 27

Prayer

Let us think this morning about showing how we care for other people. Let us learn to be kind, considerate and caring.

Let us remember how St Valentine showed all these qualities. Amen.

National Curriculum cross-curricular reference

The artefacts of Valentine's Day provide lots of scope for Art.

There are many musical pieces whose themes could be linked to this date for careful listening. Short passages might be played from a selection containing: the 'Wedding March' (Mendelssohn); the Bridal Chorus from *Lohengrin* (Wagner); the *Romeo and Juliet* overture (Tchaikovsky); and music from popular shows such as *Kiss Me, Kate* and *My Fair Lady*.

English would be well served by the dramatisation of this morning's story; and by reading about other famous couples in literature, such as Samson and Delilah, Romeo and Juliet, Hiawatha and Minnehaha from the Longfellow epic, Sydney Carton and Lucie Manette from Dickens's *A Tale of Two Cities*.

27 The plot

Introduction

This morning's story is about a man who was jealous of his cousin.
This jealousy made him try to do a dreadful thing.

Story

Devadatta was a jealous man. He was a cousin of the Buddha, and as
the Buddha's wisdom became more and more famous, so Devadatta's
jealousy grew stronger.

'I'm sick of people flocking to listen to him,' thought the jealous
cousin. 'But one day I'm going to have the chance to get him out of
the way once and for all.'

Devadatta's chance came sooner than he expected.

He was preaching in a village one day when he noticed that hardly
anybody was listening to him. They were all drifting off towards the
other end of the village.

'Where are you going?' Devadatta called out.

'The great Buddha is coming,' shouted back the villagers. 'We are
going to greet him.'

This made Devadatta angrier than ever. Soon he was alone in the
village street with only some nearby elephants for company. As he
looked at the peaceful creatures a plot came suddenly into his mind.
Moving to a house behind the elephants, he found their keeper.

'Haven't you heard?' he said sharply to the man. 'The great
Buddha is coming. He doesn't want to walk all the way. Let me have
one of these elephants so that he can ride into the village.'

'Certainly,' replied the keeper. 'You're absolutely right. He must
have the best elephant I've got.'

So Devadatta took the elephant and went with it quickly to where
some monks lived.

'Quick,' he said to one of the monks, 'we're going to meet the
great Buddha, but my elephant is thirsty, he needs some rice wine.'

Devadatta watched where the monk got the rice wine – and then,
when he was alone with it, he fed the elephant several buckets of it.
As it drank, the elephant got more and more agitated and angry.
Finally, with a great trumpet, it lunged out into the main street of the
village, as Devadatta had known it would.

The village street was full and when all the people saw the

normally peaceful elephant lunging angrily and dangerously towards them they fled in terror.

Soon only two figures were left at the end of the street. These were the Buddha and his travelling companion, Ananda.

'My lord,' gasped Ananda anxiously, 'that animal is dangerous! We must get out of the way – quickly!'

The Buddha put a hand on Ananda's shoulder. 'No, my friend – we must stay.'

With all his wisdom the Buddha knew exactly what had happened. He watched the roaring, wild elephant's approach with a calm smile on his face.

When it had almost reached him and seemed more furious than ever, the Buddha slowly held up his hands. Amazingly, the elephant stopped at once, then gradually bent its front legs and lowered its head in front of the Buddha. The Buddha stroked its head and spoke to it in a calm voice.

So Devadatta's plot had failed. The villagers marvelled even more at the Buddha's calmness and wisdom and from that day on this elephant became famous and admired for miles around.

Information for the teacher

1 February 15th is the date on which Mahayana Buddhists celebrate Parinirvana. This is the festival commemorating the death of the Buddha, when he passed on to Nirvana.
2 There are interesting comparisons to be made with this story in the realms of both folk and religious stories. To choose two only, Androcles and the lion, and St Francis of Assisi could be contrasted and compared.
3 There are other stories of the Buddha and an elephant (Damsel Face). The *Jataka* tales are a vast source of Buddha stories.

Hymn suggestion

Come and Praise Vol 2 'All the animals' No 80

Prayer

Let us pray this morning that we can live our lives without feeling jealous or envious of anybody else.

Let us be grateful for what we have ourselves.

Let us try to act towards other people in exactly the way we would want them to act towards us.

Let us end our prayers with some words of the Buddha: 'Earn your living in a way which is good. Avoid evil thoughts and actions and work hard.'

National Curriculum cross-curricular reference

A closer look at India – its location, climate, traditions, problems, animals, etc, could incorporate a great deal of History and Geography. Science could be involved in the different foods, and the lack of food, associated with the country. A look at more Indian stories (folk/religious) can produce a variety of starting points for English work.

28   Teamwork

Introduction

February is a month when the weather can change quickly – and dangerously. A day which has been bright and sunny can change into a night of freezing fog – something to beware of if you are on a long-distance walk.

Story

'It's a bit scary!'
   'Yeah – I'll be glad when we're home.'
   'I can't even see Michael.'
   'He's moved up ahead, he wants to be . . .'
   A shrill scream stopped the conversation. It tore through the mist and sleet high up in the hills of the Peak District National Park, where the boy scouts had gone for their hike. The scoutmaster pushed past the tired boys and dashed ahead to where the scream had come from. Following him, the boys helped him search, but it was no use – fourteen-year-old Michael Parsons had simply disappeared.

The party had set off for their hike that morning, 17th February, but the bad weather had closed in before they could get home. The dense fog had them all worried, even before Michael's disappearance.

'Come on, lads,' said the scoutmaster. 'I know we're on the right track and I know that where it meets the road there's a telephone box. We must get help.'

A short while later, to the boys' great relief, the party reached the road. The call for help brought an immediate response. Soon the scouts were met by a police car. In it were Inspector Guest of the local police, and Mr Heardman, an expert on the local area.

'Right,' said Inspector Guest. 'The local mountain rescue team have been called out, the Land-Rover radio truck and ambulance is on its way. But we must know where to search.'

'But it was so foggy, we don't know whereabouts on the trail Michael was lost,' said one of the boys.

'Think carefully,' said Mr Heardman to the scoutmaster. 'There are several danger spots on that route. Think carefully about any other sounds you heard.'

'Well,' said the scoutmaster doubtfully, 'we heard Michael's scream, then the sounds of him falling and stones scattering . . . and I think I also heard water . . . and there was a lot of ice and snow about.'

Mr Heardman thought carefully for a minute.

'That sounds to me like Kinder Downfall,' he said. 'There's always water there, and snow and ice when it's cold. That's the place to start the search.'

Leaving the scouts in safe hands, the rescue team set off to search for Michael. Wary of the dangers of thick mist, ice and snow, the team reached the rocky wall of Kinder Downfall and began their inch-by-inch torchlight search in the bitter winter night.

They were almost ready to give up when the torch of Derek Figg suddenly picked out a crumpled figure on a ledge.

'He's here! Careful, he needs help.'

'Coming.'

'Get the stretcher forward.'

'Keep your torch on him, Derek.'

The well-drilled team moved swiftly into action and soon Michael was being stretchered to safety.

Later, from the warmth and safety of his hospital bed, Michael told his story.

'I just slipped over the side,' he said, 'hit my head and blacked out.

When I came to I couldn't stand on one leg, and one of my arms was just dangling . . . I must have passed out again.'

Inspector Guest told how Michael had not uttered one sound despite the terrible pain he must have been in during his rescue.

'He's a brave lad,' said the policeman.

But the 'brave lad', and his parents, knew that without the expert local knowledge of Mr Heardman, and the skill and courage of the mountain rescue team, he would never have survived.

Information for the teacher

1 The party had set out from the village of Hayfield in Derbyshire for their expedition, in 1957. Their difficulties started during the afternoon of 17th February, and Michael was not found until 5.15 am on the morning of 18th February.

2 The *Pets Today* pack, published by Pedigree Petfoods Education Centre, Waltham-on-the-Wolds, Melton Mowbray, Leicestershire LE14 4RS, contains a detailed interview with David Riley of the Langdale and Ambleside Mountain Rescue Team.

Hymn suggestion

Come and Praise Vol 1 'Lost and found' No 57

Prayer

Let us pray this morning for those brave people who help when there are accidents on land, at sea or in the air.

Let us give thanks for the qualities of trust, reliance and courage which enable people to work so successfully in rescue teams.

National Curriculum cross-curricular reference

Geography is a useful link in establishing the location of the Peak District and the weather conditions which make it dangerous. Science and Technology could both be involved in considering the mechanics of a rescue operation – practicalities such as communication, resources, requirements, lifting of injured people, etc.

Dramatic possibilities are also obvious in connection with this story, and PE or Science could investigate muscles and other parts of the body used for walking, climbing, pulling.

29 The man whom everybody liked

Introduction

Is there anybody you know whom everybody likes? If so, then this person must have very special qualities – like the man this morning's story is about.

Story

George Peabody was born in a little town in the United States of America. The town was called South Danvers and George was born on 18th February 1795.

The Peabody family was very poor and by the time he was eleven years old George was already working for a grocer in town. Obviously he had had very little time to go to school.

As George grew older, he joined another man called Elisha Riggs and they opened a store selling general goods. Business was good. George was a hard worker, and when Elisha died George opened other shops all over the country and became rich.

'I'm not bothered about big houses and fancy clothes,' thought George to himself, 'but I would like to make sure other folks can benefit from my good fortune.'

So George set off alone on horseback to visit Red Indians who were considered highly dangerous by other people. Like everybody else, the Indians trusted George. He sold them useful goods at fair prices and went out of his way to be of help if they were in any kind of trouble.

George went on helping people, giving money away and being a friend to all. His fame spread right across the United States.

One day George had an idea. 'My ancestors came from England. I wonder what it's like there?' he thought. 'Well, there's only one way to find out – I'll go.'

When George arrived in London in 1837, he had two equally strong feelings. He loved the city, the bustle of the streets, the friendliness – but he hated the slums in which desperately poor people lived miserable lives.

'Hmm – this looks like something I should help with,' he thought.

George began to use his money to find areas where he could build flats to house the thousands of poor people who were living in dreadful hovels. He hired the best architects he could find to design the flats and he made sure the rents to live in them were as low as they possibly could be. His name and his actions were like magic to thousands of desperately poor Londoners.

'We're going to have a proper flat.'

'It's really got a toilet in it.'

'And there are shops on the ground floor.'

'And we can dry our clothes on the roof.'

'He's a marvellous man.'

And so he was. By 1919 over 23,000 people were living in Peabody homes and George was admired by everybody – from Queen Victoria to the poorest man in the street. When a statue of George was built and unveiled in central London the streets were packed with cheering crowds saying their own Thank You to him.

Information for the teacher

1 When George Peabody died on 4th November 1869 he had given away over two million pounds to charitable causes – a staggering sum even by today's standards.

   In his latter years he spent time in both London and the USA and gave donations to Harvard, Yale, and for the education of black people in America.

   He died in England; his funeral service was held in Westminster Abbey and his body was taken back to the USA. The town of South Danvers, Massachusetts, was renamed Peabody.

2 This story could be linked to those of other philanthropists – Lord Nuffield, the Cadbury family, Dr Barnardo, Leonard Cheshire, Sue Ryder, etc.

3 'To give and not to count the cost' is a theme which pervades all religious teachings. There are therefore several appropriate quotations to supplement this story.

   Regarding George Peabody himself, Ecclesiasticus 44, 1–2, is appropriate: 'Let us now sing the praises of famous men; the heroes of our nation's history.'

   Other 'giving' references could include:

   'The beggar was given a horse. He did not want a horse, only a meal.' (Japanese proverb)

   'When you help people, don't let your right hand know what

your left hand is doing: help people without others noticing it.'
(Matthew 6, 2–3)

'He is best loved who does most good to other creatures.' (Islamic saying)

'Give as generously as you can and share people's sorrows.' (Adapted from Ecclesiasticus 4)

'Take a real interest in ordinary people.' (From a letter from St Paul to the Christians in Rome)

Hymn suggestion

Come and Praise Vol 2 'You shall go out with joy' No 98

Prayer

Dear God,
In thanking you for those people who help us, let us remember, and think about, some words from the Bible: 'Let us never tire of doing good, for if we do not slacken our efforts we shall in due time reap our harvest. Therefore, as opportunity offers, let us work for the good of all.' Amen.

(The quotation used in this prayer is from Galations 6, 9–10.)

National Curriculum cross-curricular reference

A study of urban social conditions through the ages, or from Victorian times to now is a useful, and far-reaching, History theme. History and Geography links are equally obvious in considering how George Peabody made his journeys between England and America, and how modern travel would compare.

The 'merchant' aspect of the story could bring in Maths with work on the concepts of buying, selling and making profits.

30 A great discovery

Introduction

February is the month in which the famous Cruft's Dog Show is held. You can see it every year on television when proud owners show their dogs. Today's story is about a dog.

Story

In 1916 the First World War had been raging for two years. Every day in the trenches men were killed or injured by flying bullets and exploding shells.

Meanwhile, far from the fighting, in England, France and Germany, doctors and nurses were working desperately to try and help wounded soldiers to recover from their awful experiences.

One doctor who was busy with this work was Klaus Rimmer. He lived in Germany and he had strong ideas about how the injured men should be treated.

'Apart from the right medicine we should try and give them peace in beautiful surroundings,' he said.

Of course, if the soldier had been blinded in the war he could never see such surroundings, and Klaus felt very sorry for one of his blind patients, a man called Captain Fleitel.

One day Klaus was sitting in his office writing up some notes. He paused and looked out of the window. There he saw the tall figure of Captain Fleitel, moving slowly and hesitantly across the huge, beautiful lawn. After every few steps Fleitel paused and took a deep breath. Then summoning up his courage and putting his arms out in front of him he edged slowly forward again. Dr Rimmer sat admiring the courage of the poor soldier, when suddenly he felt a prick of alarm. Because the lawn was so big Fleitel had got more and more confident and was moving a little more quickly – straight towards a huge oak tree.

Klaus pushed open his window and was just about to shout a warning when a strange and marvellous thing happened. Frieda, Klaus's friendly Alsatian dog, had also seen the blind soldier making his worried way across the lawn. Sensing what was going to happen, the dog bounded over the grass, stopped beside Captain Fleitel and, rubbing its body against his legs, stood between him and the tree.

As the astonished doctor watched, the blind soldier reached down and gently took hold of the dog's collar. Frieda then moved slowly forward, led the man round the tree, and then up a narrow path between two flower beds.

From this marvellous event the wonderful idea of dogs guiding blind people was born.

Information for the teacher

1 The development of the use of guide dogs for the blind has obviously come a long way since this incident in 1916. The United States pursued the idea and in 1928 Morris Frank became the first

guide dog owner in that country. The Guide Dogs for the Blind Association was established in Britain in 1934, and its address is: Hillfields, Burghfield Common, Berkshire.

There are over 2,600 guide dog owners in Britain. Most of them own Labradors and the dogs need from six to eight months' training.

2 Two useful books on dogs in this context are: *Your Obedient Servant* by Angela Patmore (Hutchinson) and *Working Dogs* by Joan Palmer (Patrick Stephens).

3 In many ways this is a heroic story and could cause some reflection on some words from the Bible: 'Let us sing the praises of . . . the heroes of our nation's history . . . Their lives will endure for all time and their fame will never be blotted out . . . and God's people will sing their praises.' (Ecclesiasticus 44, 1–2 and 13–15)

4 Some reflections on Cruft's Dog Show might be both interesting and provocative.

Hymn suggestion

Come and Praise Vol 2 'All the animals' No 80

Prayer

Let us give thanks this morning for dogs.

Let us be grateful for those dogs who help the blind, the deaf and the lonely.

Let us give thanks for those dogs who work for the police and the army and air force.

Let us hope that all dogs everywhere are valued and cared for as they deserve to be.

National Curriculum cross-curricular reference

There seems to be some scope in this theme for Technology, and Science could be involved in investigating sight. This could be extended to consider the improvement in other senses as compensation when sight is lost.

The story is a good one to dramatise in English and it could also foster some sensitive written work.

31   *In a garden in Medina*

Introduction

When we are very tired we tend to think things like: When can I get a drink? When can I have something to eat? I wish I could have a rest.

You'll notice that 'I' is used a lot here. This morning's story makes us think about this.

Story

In the days when Muhammad the Prophet was a camel driver, lots of the long, hot journeys across the desert ended in Medina. Here there was a beautifully cool, shady garden and it was one of the first places the camel drivers headed for to get a refreshing drink and a rest.

One day Muhammad had finished a trip, and he took his camel to the garden in Medina. Making sure that his trusty animal was well fed and watered, he then made his way towards a large group of fellow camel drivers. The conversation was much the same as always.

'Did you have a good trip, Ahmad?'

'Yes, no trouble, and the cloth sold very well.'

'Did you hear about poor Abu Bakr?'

'No, what was that?'

'His camel went lame twenty miles from the city.'

'Oh that's . . .'

Suddenly, above the chatter of the drivers, Muhammad heard another noise. It was the gasping, throaty noise of a camel in great distress. Leaving the group, Muhammad moved to where a second lot of camels had been tethered. Most of them were comfortable in the shade, but one poor beast had been left out in the full blast of the scorching sun. Worse still, one look was sufficient to tell Muhammad that the creature was very old, had certainly not been given a drink and was in great discomfort and distress. The prophet hurried back to the camel drivers.

'Stop,' he commanded above their conversation.

Surprised, and a little alarmed, the drivers stopped talking and looked at Muhammad.

'What's wrong?' asked one of them, worriedly.

'You are all comfortable here,' said Muhammad. 'You are among friends, have eaten and drunk and are contented. One of you has left a camel out there – miserable, unfed, uncomfortable and distressed. Whoever it is should be ashamed.'

A young camel driver got to his feet, his head bowed.

'I'm sorry, Muhammad. It is my camel. I was so tired and thirsty that I . . . well, I was going to as soon as I . . . I just . . .'

'Stop wasting time and go and see to your animal,' said Muhammad. 'You would do well to remember that God places animals in our care. To neglect them or to be cruel to them is to insult God.'

Information for the teacher

1 The sensitive teacher will need always to be aware of the current year's Muslim calendar, which is not only based on the lunar year but also on sightings of the moon rather than on reckonings. In the first few years after this book's publication, this story can be linked with the beginning of the month of Ramadan, during which Muslims fast from dawn to sunset. In subsequent years the joyous festival of Eid-ul-Fitr, marking the end of the Ramadan fast, will have moved forward into February and the story can be linked equally successfully with this festival.

2 Muhammad believed in one God, Allah. He was a man who liked to be alone and when he was forty the Archangel Gabriel appeared before him and began to teach Muhammad God's message for the world. This message was ultimately written down in the Qur'an. Gabriel's appearance to Muhammad is celebrated during Ramadan, at the festival of Lailat-ul-Qadr, meaning 'The Night of Power'.

3 Hadith is the name given to the sayings and deeds of Muhammad which help Muslims understand more about Islam. One of these sayings is very appropriate for this assembly story: 'None of you believes until he wishes for his brother what he wishes for himself.'

Hymn suggestion

Come and Praise Vol 2 'All the animals' No 80

Prayer

Let us bow our heads this morning and listen to some of the words of the Prophet Muhammad:

'Forgive him who does you wrong; do good to him who does you wrong; always speak the truth even if it is against you.'

Let us keep silent for a little while to think about these words.

National Curriculum cross-curricular reference

The Qur'an contains 'ninety-one beautiful names of Allah' (Al-Hakim – the Wise, Al-Karin – the Generous, etc). This could be the lead in to a useful discussion with the children. Could one identify people we know with names such as these? What 'beautiful name' might we give to our parents, relatives, friends? Some writing could follow this discussion.

History and Geography could be served by locating Mecca and significant areas of the Muslim world, finding out about more prophets (Noah, Abraham, Jacob, etc), locating mosques in the neighbourhood.

Finally, for those who wish to develop Technology more extensively, a project on how Muslim dress has developed in various parts of the world would fit in well with AT1: 'investigate how needs and opportunities have led to design and technological activity in other cultures'.

32 Winkie

Introduction

There are lots of folk tales where a tiny animal helps a big one (for example, a mouse helping a lion). This morning's story, however, is a true one about a bird saving men.

Story

The RAF plane hit the sea off the coast of Scotland with a terrible crash. Desperately the four-man crew scrambled out of the wreckage and into a dinghy. The mountainous waves hurled the dinghy from side to side but this did not stop the battered men from seeing another survivor of the crash.

With her wings plastered down with oil from the crashed plane,

Winkie, the homing pigeon who had been on board, fluttered out to safety.

'Look!' cried the pilot. 'It's Winkie! Can we tie a message on her leg before she flies off?'

But the battered pigeon was in no mood to delay. Circling the dinghy only once, she steadied on a course and flew off, flapping her oily wings, into the rapidly approaching darkness.

Sixteen hours later, Sergeant Davidson of the RAF Pigeon Service was pacing the tarmac of the runway when suddenly Winkie staggered from the sky and landed beside him.

Sergeant Davidson took the exhausted bird for treatment and studied her closely while she was being cared for. Then he telephoned the officers in charge of the search for the plane.

'Sir,' said Sergeant Davidson, 'Winkie, the homing pigeon from that plane which is missing, has arrived here. From her condition I would guess that she has flown between 120 and 140 miles.'

Immediately the officer received this message he leaped into action.

'We've been searching too far out,' he yelled to his second in command. 'Get the rescue planes to look about 120 miles off the coast.'

Within hours the four exhausted men in the dinghy had been rescued and were on their way to hospital – saved by a pigeon.

Information for the teacher

1 The plane which crashed was a Beaufort – on 23rd February 1942. Several planes at this time carried trained homing pigeons to which it was hoped survivors could attach messages detailing their location. This, however, was the first rescue successfully completed due to the efforts of a homing pigeon.

2 Winkie later received the Dickin medal (the animal equivalent of the VC) for bravery.

3 The use of pigeons for sending military messages was certainly not new – Hannibal used them in 218 BC, as did the Greeks and Romans.

4 The courage and achievement of this pigeon was especially noteworthy because almost its entire journey was made in darkness and Winkie, like all pigeons, disliked flying in the dark. She was also in far from good condition after the crash.

Hymn suggestion

Come and Praise Vol 1 'The journey of life' No 45

Prayer

Dear God,
Let us give thanks for all the small creatures of the world. Give us the opportunity to admire their shape and form and to give thanks for the creatures who help us. Amen.

National Curriculum cross-curricular reference

The homing instincts of pigeons is still not fully understood but a great deal of Science and Maths work could be done on subjects like routes, distances, times. Birds could also be studied in more detail – for example, why and how they are so well equipped to fly.

33 Doing what is best

Introduction

This morning's story is about danger – and how a mother did what she thought was best for her baby.

Story

Many years ago the Hebrew people were ruled over by the Egyptians. The Egyptian king, who was called the Pharaoh, made the Hebrews work as slaves. They made bricks, did building jobs and laboured in the fields. They were cruelly treated.
   'We've still got a problem with these Hebrews,' said the Pharaoh one day.
   'What is that, Majesty?' asked one of his ministers.
   'There are too many of them,' replied the Pharaoh. 'We've got all the workers we need and if Hebrew boys keep being born as they are, there will soon be more Hebrews than Egyptians. Then we could have trouble.'

'Yes, Majesty,' replied the minister, wondering what the Pharaoh had in mind. He soon found out.

'We'll keep the girls,' said the Pharaoh, stroking his chin, 'but every Hebrew boy who is born from now on will be thrown into the River Nile to die.'

The minister was shocked but he knew that the Pharaoh was cruel enough to make this plan work.

So began a terrifying time for Hebrew mothers.

One of them, who had a baby boy called Moses, hid the child for three months. But every day she feared the arrival of soldiers who would find and kill the child. Finally she decided that she must do something drastic. She told her plan to Moses's sister, Miriam.

'We can't hide him any more,' she said. 'This is what we'll do. We'll coat his cradle of reeds with pitch to make it waterproof, then we'll put the basket near the reeds on the river where the king's daughter often comes to bathe.'

'But what then?' asked Miriam.

'I've heard the princess loves children. When she finds Moses you can go up to her and say you know a very good woman who will look after the baby for her if she wants to keep it.'

'And of course *you* are . . .'

'That's right. I'll go and look after the baby for the princess. That way I'll be able to save my son's life, *and* look after him.'

'It sounds like a good plan,' said Miriam.

It was, because it worked out exactly as Moses's mother hoped it would.

Information for the teacher

1 Teachers who wish to refer to the Bible with regard to this story will find references to the Children of Israel growing in number and wealth in Genesis 47, 27. A verse describing how cruelly the Pharaoh treated the Israelites is Exodus 1, 22.

Exodus 2 tells the story of Moses in these early days, and it may be useful to note the significance of his name: Moses means 'Drawn Out' (of the water).

2 There are dates in February which can be related to this story for different reasons. Another massacre took place at Glencoe in Scotland on 13th February 1692. This was when the Campbells murdered the Macdonalds.

On a more positive line of 'rescuing something from difficult circumstances', Christopher Wren died on 25th February 1723. He virtually recreated a great deal of London (including over 50 churches) after the Great Fire of London in 1666.

Hymn suggestion

Come and Praise Vol 2 'What about being old Moses' No 81

Prayer

Let us bow our heads and think this morning about Moses. He became a great leader of people and God told him of rules that were necessary for Christians.

Let us remember how important it is to respect our mothers and fathers; to be a good neighbour at all times; and to make sure we don't ever do anything which is hurtful to someone else.

National Curriculum cross-curricular reference

The various elements of this story make it both an appropriate and powerful one for drama. Written English could also feature in observations and retelling. The construction of a waterproof receptacle such as described in the story could form the basis of a project in Technology.

34 *Welcome to a stranger*

Introduction

'To give is to receive' is a well-known saying. This morning's story is one which helps us to understand this saying.

Story

Eumaeus looked at the dogs as they lay round his feet. Another day's work was over and he was tired. He usually felt tired at this time of the day. His thoughts went back to when he was young and Odysseus was king. Those were the great days. Now the king was long gone and with nobody in charge of the country there was too much selfishness and arguing.

'What is it, boys?'

Eumaeus asked the question of his dogs. Their ears had gone up and they were growling in the back of their throats. There was somebody outside!

Quickly, Eumaeus got to his feet and opened the door. The dogs bounded out and were soon barking furiously. As Eumaeus moved closer he saw that they were surrounding an old man in ragged clothes.

'Back, dogs, back!' cried Eumaeus.

The old man looked up gratefully.

'You look tired sir,' said Eumaeus. 'Come into my cottage and share my meal with me.'

'Thank you,' said the stranger.

So the two men went into the cottage and shared the meal Eumaeus had prepared for himself. When the stranger had finished he wiped his mouth and spoke.

'Thank you for the meal. You were indeed kind to share it with me.'

'It was a pleasure,' replied Eumaeus. 'But tell me, why do you come to this land?'

'I have heard it is a splendid place,' replied the stranger.

'Ha, it was once! We had a young king called Odysseus, but he sailed away to a war. He never returned and we have given him up for dead.'

The stranger then gave an odd smile. He opened the side of his ragged cloak and spoke again.

'Look, my friend.'

Puzzled, Eumaeus moved closer and saw the deep scar on the man's side.

'It can't be . . .'

'It is, Eumaeus. You remember when I got this wound? We were fighting side by side for our country.'

'My Lord . . . you're back!'

So Eumaeus and the returned king Odysseus embraced each other. Odysseus smiled with pleasure as he thought of the kind Eumaeus who had given him such a welcome – without even knowing who he was.

Information for the teacher

1 *The Myths of Greece and Rome* by H A Guerber (Harrap) is a book first published in 1907. Many reprints later, it is still a valuable assembly resource.

2 This is another story well suited to the quotation: 'It is not what you have that matters. It is what you do with what you have.' These words were spoken by Sir Wilfred Grenfell who was born on 28th February 1865. Like Eumaeus in the story, he was a man of great kindness and consideration – as evidenced by his famous missionary work with the Eskimos in Labrador.

Hymn suggestion

Come and Praise Vol 1 'When I need a neighbour' No 65

Prayer

Dear God,
Help us to remember that it is the qualities within a person which make him or her so special. Amen.

National Curriculum cross-curricular reference

Stories from the *Myths of Greece and Rome* are of course the basis of many junior school History lessons. The location of these sources could embrace Geography, and many of them are well suited for drama and discussion in English.

March

35 Guard my treasure

Introduction

'Honesty is the best policy' is a very old saying but it is a good one to follow – as this morning's story shows.

Story

'It's such a shame – but the truth is, I can't really trust him'.

As he said these words to himself, Giovanni the rich merchant looked out of one of the windows of his fine house. Down below in the garden Alfredo played with the family dog.

Alfredo had called on Giovanni many months ago.

'I'm down on my luck,' he said. 'Could you give me some work? You'll find I am a very good worker.'

Feeling sorry for the nice looking young man, Giovanni had taken him in. Alfredo did indeed prove an excellent worker and in no time at all he was Giovanni's right-hand man. He ran the estate, paid the workers, bought and sold fine cloth, and did it all with a smile on his face.

But Giovanni hadn't got to be a rich man by being foolish. He soon found out that a bale of the finest cloth had 'disappeared'; some of the workers complained about not getting their proper wages; odd valuable items were no longer to be seen about the house.

'None of these things happened before Alfredo came,' thought Giovanni sadly. 'I'm sure he's stealing from me – so we shall have to see.'

That night Giovanni asked Alfredo to join him for the evening meal.

'Alfredo,' started the merchant seriously, 'I have to go away on business for a few days and I need to be sure that everything is safe at home. I'm going to put my most precious jewels and possessions in a large chest. Will you look after it for me while I am away?'

'Of course, Giovanni,' replied the handsome Alfredo, with one of his most charming smiles. 'It will be a pleasure. You can sleep well at night knowing everything is safe with me.'

Two days later two servants carried a large and very heavy chest into Alfredo's room. Behind them Giovanni and Alfredo walked along in deep conversation.

'Guard it well,' said Giovanni. 'My fortune lies in that chest.'

As he spoke, he pointed to the large box which was sealed with two large seals.

'Don't worry,' replied Alfredo. 'It will be locked in my room and neither I nor anybody else will touch it until you get back.'

Giovanni went on his way. A little over a week went by and then one hot and sunny morning he and his fellow horseman were seen approaching the house up the long and dusty driveway.

'Alfredo! It's good to see you again,' said Giovanni. 'That was a very successful trip. How has everything been here?'

'All right.'

'You don't sound very happy,' replied Giovanni glancing at the surly looking Alfredo. 'What's the matter?'

For a moment, Alfredo said nothing. Then his irritation and impatience got the better of him.

'It's you . . . you said you trusted me. You told me you were leaving all your riches in my care. But that chest was just full of heavy stones. It was . . .' Alfredo stopped. He had realised his mistake – but it was too late.

Information for the teacher

1 Useful calendar references for this story could be the deaths of the Wesley brothers, both of whom died in March. Both were great advocates of Christian virtues and John, who died on 2nd March 1791, not only founded Methodism but was a pioneer in 'taking Christianity to the people'.

 Charles Wesley died on 29th March 1788 and is mostly remembered for his hymns. He believed that the words of hymns should be as simple and honest as possible so that they would appeal to ordinary people.

2 'Honesty' is a theme which can be used to incorporate folk stories of all cultures, and modern, true-life stories as well. There are plenty of thought-provoking sayings which are relevant too, for example: 'Be worthy of a reputation' (Confucius); and 'The world is preserved by three things: truth, justice, peace' (Jewish saying).

Hymn suggestion

Come and Praise Vol 2 'Make us worthy, Lord' No 94

Prayer

Dear God,
Teach us to be honest in our dealings with other people. Help us not
to tell lies and give us strength to be honest about admitting our
mistakes. Help us to be honest in saying we think someone is wrong
even when doing this makes us unpopular. Amen.

National Curriculum cross-curricular reference

Both the story and the prayer give rise to discussion topics. Children
of primary-school age are well aware of 'peer group pressure' and
how difficult it is to express an honest opinion when this is a minority
or even individual viewpoint. A discussion on this could then be
illustrated by dramatised situations.

   In Technology the question of 'seals' could be investigated
practically – What are effective seals? Can they be broken and
repaired without any damage being apparent? Are seals still used
today? If so, on what and how?

36   More!

Introduction

Imagine that you are at a birthday party. The person who has cut the
cake hasn't made a very good job of it and the slices are uneven.
When yours arrives it looks absolutely lovely – but your neighbour's
is bigger. How do you feel about this?

Story

Oscar had a good home and was well fed. But, like most dogs, he
was always on the lookout for anything extra to eat. One day he was
passing the local butcher's on one of his morning adventures.

'Hi, Oscar,' shouted the butcher, who knew him well. 'Got a treat for you here. Catch.'

So saying, he threw a nice juicy piece of meat in the dog's direction.

Oscar caught it in his mouth, and wagged his tail to show his thanks. 'Right, I'm going to take this back to my garden where I can enjoy it in peace,' he thought to himself.

Now, Oscar lived in a cottage just outside the village. To get to it he had to cross over a bridge. Beneath the bridge ran a very slow-moving stream. On this particular morning it was very calm and the water was hardly moving at all.

'Nearly home,' thought Oscar as he trotted up onto the bridge. Then, looking over the side of the bridge, he saw something underneath – another dog with a huge piece of meat in his mouth.

'His piece of meat is far bigger than mine,' thought Oscar. He stopped and looked down again. The dog looked straight back at him.

Oscar growled in the back of his throat. 'Why should he have a bigger piece than me? I'm going to do something about that!'

With a snarl, Oscar leaped off the bridge to attack the dog below him. He hit the water with a tremendous splash, and his piece of meat swirled away as the water shot up his nose and into his mouth.

For a few seconds he floundered about, puzzled and angry. Of course, if he'd been a human being he would have known that what he had seen was his reflection – but his greed for more had cost him what he had in the first place.

Information for the teacher

1 There are some interesting March connections on the theme of 'food'. The first packaged food was sold in the USA on 6th March 1930, and Kellogg's Corn Flakes first appeared on the 7th in 1897. Johnny Appleseed, the legendary apple tree planter of the USA, died on 11th March 1847. A useful link with dogs is that 10th March 1886 was the occasion of the first Cruft's Dog Show in London.

2 This story could be used as one of a small series which involve 'reflections'. There is a well-known Chinese folk tale in which a wife finds a mirror in her husband's belongings. On looking in it she sees 'another woman' and accuses him accordingly!

In Greek mythology Narcissus was so impressed with the beauty he saw in his reflection that he jumped into the water to touch it and was drowned – hence 'narcissism' to mean 'the love of oneself'.

The children will be aware of the significance of the mirror in the Snow White story.

Thus a strong moral link could be established between a thread of stories around the same theme.

Hymn suggestion

Come and Praise Vol 1 'Who put the colours in the rainbow?' No 12

Prayer

Let us pray this morning that we may see ourselves as we really are. Let us recognise our faults and try to do something about them. Let us not concern ourselves too much about the faults of others. Amen.

National Curriculum cross-curricular reference

Reflections and mirrors are areas very much bound up with National Curriculum Science and the stories suggested here could add another dimension to practical work in this context.

Technology could also be involved and there is a great deal of scope in both Music and Art, where sounds and illustration could be 'mirrored'. There is plenty of scope in English for researching other stories which 'reflect' this theme. These could then be listened to and discussed. 'The drawing of conclusions' would be a useful theme here.

37 *This month*

Introduction

Out of doors, March is one of the most exciting months of the year. The days are starting to get longer and there is the feeling of things awakening on the land, in the air and in water.

This month

March is a good month for saying to somebody: 'Go outside, look and listen.'

Some of the things you could look for are hares. This is the time of year when male hares leap about, box each other and beat their hind legs on the ground. If you are lucky you could see them doing this – and the females looking on in the distance.

March is a good month to look out for birds and their nests. With many trees still bare it is easy to see that the birds – rooks in particular – are busy, noisy and fussy. Rooks nest in big trees and are notorious thieves who steal nest-building twigs whenever they get the chance.

For the careful watcher it is interesting to make a list of how birds differ in their approach to nest-building. Tawny owls, for instance, make only a very simple nest – a saucer-shaped thing made of bits of bark and the remains of owl pellets. These can be found in hollow trees. The peewit (lapwing) nests on open ground and its nest is little more than a hollow scraped in the ground. Sparrows work at building their nests in holes in walls and under the eaves of barns, sheds and houses. They use plenty of straw and feathers for their nests.

Other things to look out for in March include the activity in and around ponds. Duckweed plants start to spread over the ponds, and in and around the water frogs, toads and newts can be found. Butterflies can be seen trying their wings and in different places a variety of flowers start to appear.

Marsh marigolds bring a yellow pattern to the sides of streams; bluebells and anemones start to show and, if it is warm, look out for the first star-white flowers of stitchwort.

So much for 'looking' in March; now what about 'listening'? The following are sounds you could expect to hear. The cock snipe swoops in flight at this time of year and when this happens the wind rushes through its wing- and tail-feathers – making a definite 'drumming' sound. Listen too for birds with 'whistles'. The peewit has a long whistle and to spot it you should look for a glossy brown and white bird who looks as if he is tumbling about when flying. The blackbird is another whistler and he is black with a yellow beak.

It is hard to miss the noisy and often angry 'cawing' of the rooks in March. Perhaps a more interesting sound is the quickfire 'rat-a-tat-tat' of the woodpecker at work.

The weather in March can change very quickly. Wind, rain, frost, snow and sun are all equally possible but it is cheering to remember the old saying: 'When March comes in like a lion it goes out like a lamb.'

Information for the teacher

1 In connection with an assembly like this some teachers may want to develop some symbolism as well: flowers like Lent lilies, for instance, supposedly symbolise betrayal when yellow and purity when white. The lungwort (*Pulmonaria officinalis*) is an early spring flower whose hanging bells are blue with a touch of red. Old traditions claim the blue represents Mary's robe, splashed with the blood of Jesus from when she stood beneath the cross at his crucifixion. Other names for this flower are Soldiers and Sailors and Our Lady's Violets. Another flower symbolising Mary's blue robes is the anenome.

2 Another old traditional story which children enjoy hearing at this time of year concerns Lady Day (25th March). In Belgium it was believed that on this day God commanded the world to be silent. Everything obeyed his command – except the cuckoo. As a punishment, this bird was never allowed to have a nest of its own or to stay in any one place too long.

3 Notable feasts which often occur in March are: Mothering Sunday which is the fourth Sunday in Lent and was traditionally the day on which apprentices were given time off to visit their mothers; Passion Sunday which is the fifth Sunday in Lent and commemorates Christ's suffering in the Garden of Gethsemane; Palm Sunday, which commemorates Jesus's triumphal entry into Jerusalem.

Hymn suggestion

Come and Praise Vol 2 'Sing, people, sing' No 110

Prayer

Let us bow our heads and listen to the last verse of our hymn this morning:

> Sing, people, sing,
> And follow in a ring,
> Praise to God for all we do,
> Marching, seeing, hearing, too;

Sing, people, sing,
Sing, people, sing.
(Traditional)

National Curriculum cross-curricular reference

There are tremendous possibilities for scientific and environmental studies stemming from outdoor observations at this time of year. English could be well served by many of the symbolic and legendary stories and there is plenty of scope for Art – particularly if subjects like 'Easter Eggs' and 'Easter Gardens' are to be developed here.

The 'sounds' described in this assembly could lead on to some improvised music with the children. Appropriate classical music considerations are: *Appalachian Spring* (Aaron Copland), *Rite of Spring* (Stravinsky), and the Easter Hymn from *Cavalleria Rusticana* by Mascagni.

38 One hot Australian day

Introduction

Australia is a huge country. Away from the cities many of its roads are not good and driving lorries in intense heat is a hard, and sometimes dangerous, way of earning a living.

Story

Sandor Gubonyi came out of the hospital on that late March day feeling lucky, as well as glad to be alive. As he came down the steps he saw a group of people waiting for him. With them, and barking excitedly, was his dog Bimbo. As Sandor ruffled the dog's ears he thought of their first meeting weeks ago . . .

The huge truck bounced and rattled over the potholed road in the West Australian outback. The heat was tremendous and Sandor constantly wiped the sweat from his brow as he fought to control the twisting, leaping steering wheel.

'Boy, will I be glad to finish this trip,' he muttered to himself, as another deep pothole sent a crushing shudder up his arms. Then it happened – the truck hit the deepest rut yet, swerved violently, and, with a scream of tearing metal, crashed on its side and slid sideways along the rough road surface.

When it finally stopped Sandor found himself trapped beneath part of the overturned lorry. 'I've got to get out of here,' he said aloud through gritted teeth. 'I've got to.'

The pain in his injured back was terrible but, inch by inch, the driver edged his way out from under the lorry. Finally, he could move no farther. Then he realised that he had more serious problems.

'The water carrier,' muttered Sandor. The crash had taken care of it and without water he knew he would not survive long in the intense heat.

'Maybe I won't have to wait that long,' Sandor thought as he looked upwards. Blackening the sky above him was a huge flight of swirling, cawing crows. Alerted by the crash and with the sight of easy prey on the ground, they began to swoop lower and lower. Their hideous cries and savage beaks were terrifying and Sandor buried his head in his hands and waited for the first strike.

Then, a new noise rose above the cries of the birds. A dog was barking. Cautiously, Sandor opened his eyes and peered over a protective arm. Leaping and barking at the diving crows was a dog. It was the sort of dog that many local cattlemen used and it looked as dusty and worn as Sandor felt.

'Go on, chum, good on you,' muttered the driver encouragingly.

Again and again the dog fought off the birds until at last, with their meal now taking too much effort, the crows flew off to find other prey. When they had gone the dog came and lay beside Sandor and gently licked his face.

'If we ever get out of this you and I are never going to be parted,' said the driver, 'and I'm going to call you Bimbo.'

The story had a happy ending. Before too long a helicopter found the overturned lorry, and driver and dog were airlifted to hospital. When Bimbo's story was told he became famous. Not only was his courage written about in all the newspapers but he was awarded the Australian Dogs' Victoria Cross. Now, instead of being a stray in the bush, he was a celebrity!

Sure enough, when Sandor came out of hospital the two were reunited. 'After all, I wouldn't be here without him,' said the driver, now fully recovered.

Information for the teacher

1 Driving long-distance lorries in Australia remains a very tough job. Enormous distances, a demanding climate, lack of dual carriageways and a sparse population all contribute to this.
2 'Journeys' is a theme which could be expanded from this story. Joseph's journey with Mary prior to the first Christmas is a very famous Biblical one. Another from the same source is the Israelites' journey from Egypt. This could begin with Moses's instructions at the burning bush (Exodus 3) right through the ten plagues (Exodus 8) to the crossing of the Red Sea (Exodus 14) and the journey on into the desert (Exodus 16).

One of the most remarkable journeys of both ancient and modern times is the Muslim *hajj*. This is the journey to Mecca which Muslims have been making for over thirteen centuries. From all over the Muslim world, up to two million pilgrims make this journey annually. Before arriving at Mecca all put on the simple *ihram* costume. For men this is two pieces of unsewn white cloth; for women it is a simple gown with the face unveiled. These costumes, worn by everyone regardless of how rich or poor, important or humble, emphasise the fact that everyone is of equal importance in the eyes of Allah.

Hymn suggestion

Come and Praise Vol 2 'The sun burns hot' No 77

Prayer

Let us think this morning about journeys. Let us pray for those whose work causes them to make long and difficult journeys. May they be kept safe and well until they return to their homes and families. Amen.

National Curriculum cross-curricular reference

Two large areas of geographical study are offered if both the set story and the journey to Mecca are followed up. Research into the Australian story (via climate, distance, population, etc) would emphasise one of the difficulties in transporting food in Australia. The Plain of Arafat to which the thousands of Muslims go on their *hajj* could be located, and more research done into the background.

The value of water to sustain life could be examined in more detail from a scientific point of view.

39　Tell the truth

Introduction

This morning's story is a very old one. It describes how, when people want to do something which is very wrong, they are sometimes stopped in mysterious ways.

Story

The farmer was very busy sowing wheat when he saw the little group moving towards him. As they got nearer he saw a man, a woman with what looked like a tiny baby, and a donkey. The farmer was a friendly man so he called out to the strangers.

'Hello there! You look tired and hot. Why not rest here in the shade awhile? You're welcome to share some of my food and drink.'

The couple stopped.

'That's very kind of you,' said the man. 'My name is Joseph. This is my wife Mary and this is our baby son.'

'Well,' said the farmer, 'I'm pleased to meet you – but, if you don't mind my asking, why are you trying to make such haste in the heat of the day?'

Mary looked at her husband as if to say, 'Why don't you tell him?'

Joseph looked at the farmer's honest face and then he told him that soldiers were trying to kill Jesus and that this could give the farmer trouble later on.

'Why,' said the farmer, 'that's absolutely terrible. You must get away! What a dreadful thing.'

'Thank you again,' said Joseph. 'We will get on our way now. But I must warn you that Herod's soldiers are everywhere. It's quite likely that they'll come here and ask if you've seen us.'

'Oh dear,' said the farmer. 'I'm no good at telling lies. What on earth will I say?'

'Well,' replied Joseph, 'you must tell them the truth – but tell them what you were doing when you saw us.'

As the couple and child went on their way the farmer got back to sowing his wheat. When he had finished he went home to bed.

The next morning the farmer could hardly believe his eyes when he awoke. There in the field in which he had been working was a mass of tall, ripe wheat just ready for harvesting!

'But that's impossible, it can't be . . .'

He was still looking out in amazement when, at the edge of the field, he noticed a group of soldiers urging their horses on cruelly. Within minutes they had reached his house and were hammering on the door.

'Now you,' snarled the leader of the soldiers when the farmer had opened the door. 'We've got some questions for you, and it will be a very bad job for you if you don't tell the truth. We're looking for some people.'

The soldier gave a very good description of Joseph and Mary. When he had done this he asked, 'Have you seen these people?'

'Oh yes,' said the farmer. 'I have certainly seen them.'

'Ah,' said the soldier, 'at last! Now then, man, when did you see them?'

'Oh, it was the day I was sowing wheat seeds in this field,' answered the farmer truthfully.

The soldier turned to look at the field of ripe wheat, then he looked again at the farmer.

'The day you sowed the wheat, why that must have been . . .' With a snort of disgust the soldier stormed away. 'They can't be anywhere near here!' he called out to his men.

Information for the teacher

1 The three wise men went originally to Jerusalem. Having seen the star in the sky as the sign of the birth of a king, and knowing that the royal palace was at Jerusalem, they thought they would find the new king there.

Herod received them and, wondering who this new king of the Jews could be, he questioned them carefully. He then told them that when they did find the new king they should let him know where he was so he could go to worship him too. Having found Jesus in Bethlehem, however, they were told by God in a dream that they should not give Herod this information. By the same means Joseph was told to take Mary and Jesus away.

Herod was furious when the wise men did not report back to him. When he heard of the birth in Bethlehem he ordered the death of all baby boys under two years old who lived there, or nearby. (Matthew 2 is useful for source material.)

2 The calendar link for this day is that early spring is the time when crops start to appear.

Hymn suggestion

Come and Praise Vol 2 'And ev'ryone beneath the vine' No 149

Prayer

Let us think of the many mysteries in life which we don't understand. Let us remember the words of a very old saying: 'God moves in mysterious ways, his wonders to perform.'

National Curriculum cross-curricular reference

Science could be involved here in considering essential requirements for the growth of crops. Such a consideration could involve practical 'growing' experiments in the classroom.

This theme of 'good defeats evil' could lead to discussions in studying the power of rulers like Herod in the past, and the growth of democracy in a country like Britain.

40 *Not quite perfect*

Introduction

Imagine that you are going to get a present. It is the best computer that money can buy, with every possible gadget. You would expect it to be perfect, wouldn't you?

Story

The twins had never seen their mother so excited. Both Floella and Simon listened, fascinated, while Mrs Garbutt spoke to her husband.

'It's amazing, Clive,' she said. 'It's really amazing.'

'Well, you've always been kind to her . . . you deserve it!'

'But . . . being able to buy the best!'

For years Mrs Garbutt had looked after the old lady next door as well as she could. She'd done her shopping, made her regular meals, mowed the lawn . . .

'And then she said to me that she'd been left quite a lot of money and she wanted me to have a special present. I could choose something and have the very best.'

'Well, what have you decided to get?' asked Dad.

'You know, I've always wanted a real Persian carpet – just a small one to put in the middle of the room. That's what I'm going to choose. On Saturday we'll go into that special carpet shop on the outskirts of the town.'

When Saturday came Mr and Mrs Garbutt and the twins drove out to Suleiman Carpets. The shop was like nothing the children had ever seen before.

'It's like being in a strange country,' whispered Floella.

'Yeah,' agreed Simon. 'It even smells different, doesn't it?'

'And have you seen those funny little brass things everywhere?'

'You mean – like teapots?'

Meanwhile, Mum and Dad were talking to a salesman.

'We're looking for a small Persian carpet.'

'Of course – would you like a coffee while you're choosing – and a drink for the children, perhaps?'

The twins explored the mysterious shop thoroughly until, about half an hour later, Mum had decided which carpet she wanted.

'It's very expensive but it's just what I want,' she said to the salesman. 'It's absolutely perfect.'

'No, madam – it's not.'

'Sorry? I don't understand.'

'I said it's not perfect.'

'But if it's not perfect how can you be charging all this money for it?'

'Let me explain,' went on the salesman. 'Persian carpets are the finest in the world – there can be no doubt about that. But the people who weave the carpets believe that only God, or Allah as they say, can create a perfect thing. Therefore in every carpet they make, no matter what a work of art it is, they make a tiny deliberate mistake.'

'And this carpet has such a mistake?'

'Look,' said the salesman.

Then, with his finger, he traced round one of the beautiful intricate patterns on the carpet – and pointed out how one tiny, tiny bit of the pattern didn't quite fit.

'Well, we would never have spotted that!' gasped Mum.

'No madam, only an expert can find the mistake – but it is one of the ways in which we can tell if the carpet is absolutely genuine.'

'Well,' gasped Dad. 'We've certainly learned something today.'

Information for the teacher

1 Linking stories to the Muslim calendar is always tricky because of its lunar base. However, this story could be linked to the great Muslim feast of Eid-ul-Fitr which in 1993, 1994 and 1995 takes place in March.

Eid-ul-Fitr is the day which celebrates the end of fasting during the holy month of Ramadan. New clothes are worn to greet this day and a special breakfast is eaten. Prayers in the mosque on this day begin with the imam calling out: 'Allah-o-Akbar' ('Allah is the Greatest').

After worship it is a party day with family gatherings, special meals and the exchange of presents.

2 Some quotations from the Qur'an and sayings from Muhammad encapsulate the feeling behind the main point of this morning's story, for example:

'Your God is the most generous . . . who taught man what he knew not.'

'Worship Allah as if you see Him; if you do not see Him, know that he sees you.'

'Be careful of your duty to Allah.'

3 For those near enough, a visit to the Victoria and Albert Museum in London would be a useful follow-up. Among its comprehensive collection of items from the Muslim world are carpets.

Hymn suggestion

Come and Praise Vol 1 'Peace, perfect peace' No 53

Prayer

Dear God,
Although we can never be perfect, help us at all times to do our best. Teach us not to be too easily satisfied with our efforts and help us always to try and seek improvement. Amen.

National Curriculum cross-curricular reference

Geography could be involved in locating where Muslim influence is at its strongest. Finding out about local Muslim communities, where possible, could also be rewarding here.

History could be involved in looking at the growth and development of the Muslim world. In Art, a look at some examples of Islamic art could prove both interesting and stimulating, and a carpet pattern might be designed, with the possibility of some weaving to follow up.

41   *The healing of the blind man*

Introduction

One of the most noticeable things about the stories of Jesus is that he was always trying to help people.

Story

Jesus and his disciples did a lot of travelling around. For a time they stayed with two sisters who were called Martha and Mary.

The house where Martha and Mary lived was in a village called Bethany. This village was near to the city of Jerusalem. One day Jesus and his friends decided to go for a walk. The disciples knew that something interesting almost always happened when they went out for walks.

As usual, it was hot and the road was very dry and dusty. As they walked along, they heard a man's voice calling out in the distance. When they got closer they saw that the man who was making all the noise was sitting by the side of the road. He had one hand stretched out in front of him.

'Can you help a blind man?' he called out, over and over again.

'Isn't it sad,' said Peter. 'Because he is blind all the poor man can do is beg.'

'Can you help a blind man?' the voice called out again.

Jesus stopped in front of him. He paused for a moment and then carefully spat on the ground. Then he bent down and made clay with the dust and water.

'Now, my friend,' said Jesus, 'keep still for a moment.'

Not knowing what was happening the blind man kept still and quiet.

Jesus bent down. 'This won't hurt,' he said. Then he spread the clay over the man's eyes.

'Who are you?' asked the blind man. 'Why are you doing this?'

'You are talking to Jesus,' said Peter. 'Listen carefully to what he tells you.'

'One of my friends will lead you over to a pool of water,' said Jesus. 'When you get there, carefully wash all the mud off your eyes.'

After the man had been taken to the pool, Jesus and his friends went on their way. Meanwhile the blind man slowly washed each tiny piece of mud away from his eyes. Then, holding his breath, he slowly opened one eye, and then the other.

Suddenly a great shout tore through the air.

'I can see!' shouted the man. 'I can see! I can see!'

People nearby looked round to see what all the fuss was about.

'Look – that's the blind beggar, isn't it?'

'What's he shouting about?'

'He doesn't seem blind any more.'

'How strange.'

The people went up to the man who had been blind. They formed a circle round him and jostled each other as they sought to look at him more closely.

'You're not blind any more.'

'That's amazing!'

'What happened?'

'Yes . . . come on, tell us. How come you can see now?'

The blind man looked around him. He blinked his eyes. 'It was a man called Jesus,' he said. 'He made this mud and put it on my eyes. Then he told me to go to the pool and wash it off. When I washed it off I could see. I can see – I can actually see. Isn't it wonderful?'

Information for the teacher

1 A useful address here might be Guide Dogs for the Blind Association, Hillfields, Burghfield Common, Berkshire. Two relevant and useful books are: *Working Dogs* by Joan Palmer (Patrick Stephens) and *Your Obedient Servant* by Angela Patmore (Hutchinson).

2 The original source for this Bible story is John 9, 1–41. There are other Biblical references to Jesus curing blind people: Mark 8, 24; Matthew 9, 27–31; Matthew 20, 30–34; Mark 10, 46–52.

Blindness in Biblical times was common and blind beggars lined the most-used roadways. Apart from the blindness of old age, another cause was ophthalmia (inflammation of the eye, its membranes or its lids), which was not only infectious but was also worsened by the dust and glare caused by the prevailing climate.

3 The calendar link with this story is again the focusing of attention on Jesus and his ministry, leading up to the events of the first Easter.

Hymn suggestion

Come and Praise Vol 1 'From the darkness came light' No 29

Prayer

Let us bow our heads and listen to the words of a famous prayer:
   'God our Father, guide and strengthen us by your Spirit that we may give ourselves in love and service to one another and to you.' Amen.

National Curriculum cross-curricular reference

Science could be involved in some research into sight, blindness and conditions detrimental to good sight. There is obvious scope for practical experiments here, involving light, artificial light, darkness, distance, etc. More details of the climate of the Holy Land could be studied in Geography.

42   A cause for concern

Introduction

Sometimes we need to find out why people behave as they do in certain circumstances. This morning's true story tells us a lot about life today.

Story

John and Rachid were sitting in their car outside a block of flats in a busy city on a cold March day. They were waiting for their friend Ivor.

'I wish he would hurry up,' said John.

'Yes,' replied Rachid, 'if he doesn't get a move on we'll miss the beginning of the picture.'

'Hmm. It will take us at least ten minutes to reach that car park next to the cinema.'

The two men sat chatting. It was dark outside and there were very few people about. Suddenly John noticed an old lady walking along the pavement in front of the flats. At first she was walking quite briskly but, as she got nearer, she seemed to go slower and slower. It was almost as if she was walking in thick sand.

Now Rachid was watching her too. As she got alongside the car, her knees gave way and she sank slowly to the ground.

'She's ill!' called John. 'Quick, let's go and help her.'

The two men jumped out of the car and hurried over to where the old lady sat gasping on the pavement.

'Can we help?' asked John anxiously.

'No . . . leave me alone, please,' gasped the old lady. 'I'll be all right in a minute.'

'I don't think we can do that,' replied Rachid. 'Let us get you home and call a doctor.'

'No, really, I sometimes get these breathless spells,' went on the old lady. 'Just leave me alone.'

'Certainly not,' went on John. 'We've got a car here – we'll take you straight home, or to hospital if you like.'

'What's your address?' asked Rachid.

For a moment or two the old lady looked as if she would ask them to leave again. Then, with a sigh and a sad look on her face, she said, '21, Eastville Close.'

'Oh, that's quite near,' replied John.

He and Rachid then helped the old lady into the car. She seemed much better – but very worried. Within a few minutes they were holding her and knocking on the front door of 21 Eastville Close.

'Mum!' cried the young woman who opened the door.

Soon they were all inside, and while the young woman put her mother to bed, John and Rachid waited to see if there was anything else they could do.

When the daughter came back they asked her.

'No, I don't think so,' she said. 'I've called the doctor from the bedroom telephone and he'll be round in a few minutes.'

'Oh, that's good,' said John.

'But I would like to say,' went on the young woman, 'how much I appreciate you bringing Mum home. It really was very kind of you.'

'It's the least we could do,' said Rachid. 'But, you know, it was ages before she would tell us where she lived.'

'I know,' replied the daughter. 'You see, she was frightened that if she gave her address it would be easy for you to come and rob the place when you brought her here.'

John and Rachid were shocked.

'You mean . . . she really thought we would do that?' gasped John. 'How awful.'

Information for the teacher

1 Although the names have been changed, this story happened exactly as described. As such it can stimulate a great deal of discussion with upper juniors, ranging over a wide variety of themes from 'trust' to 'our society today'.
2 All religions advocate helping one's neighbour without reservation. They do so in a variety of words:

'Out of the cotton of comparison spin a thread of contentment.' (Guru Nanak)

'There is only one race – the human race.' (Guru Gobind Singh)

'If you shut your ears when people cry for help, When you cry for help, no one will hear you.' (Proverbs 21, 13)

> 'May God keep us safe;
> May He protect us.
> Let us all work together;
> Let Him enlighten our minds.
> Let us not dislike each other.'
> (From the Hindu *Upanishads*)

Hymn suggestion

Come and Praise Vol 2 'Sad, puzzled eyes' No 74

Prayer

Dear God,
Help us to behave in a way which will allow people to rely on us and trust us.

Let us pray also for those who seek to rob and cheat other people. We pray that they may be shown how to behave with kindness and trust too. Amen.

National Curriculum cross-curricular reference

History could certainly be involved here in tracing the establishment of law and order through the ages.

There is much to discuss in an English context, and the 'concern' angle could be developed very much more in RE.

43 The idols

Introduction

All children enjoy being told that, sometimes, adults can learn from children. This morning's story is about a very wise boy called Abraham.

Story

'It's wrong,' thought Abraham, 'I just know it's all wrong.'

He was standing in his father's shop looking round. On every shelf, different sized clay statues were stacked in rows. Abraham's father made these statues and then sold them to people. The people took them to their homes and worshipped them as gods.

'It's ridiculous,' thought Abraham, as he fingered one of the clay models. 'How can people worship these things that my father makes in his back room, when there is only one God who should be worshipped?'

Continuing to walk round the shop, Abraham moved the statues from here to there, worrying all the time.

'If only my father would use his skill to make clay pots and dishes – that would be far more sensible. No good can come of making these statues.'

Finally Abraham stopped. He would have to be cruel to be kind. It was the only way to make his father see sense. With a sigh he went into the workshop and brought out a hammer. Slowly, and with tears in his eyes, for he knew how hard his father worked, he began to break each statue. Eventually there was only one statue left. It was easily the biggest in the shop. Abraham lifted it down and stood it amidst the wreckage of the others. Then he leaned the hammer beside it.

Sometime later, Abraham's father, Terah, came home. When he saw the mess in the shop he was furious. Shouting for Abraham, he pointed at the pile of broken statues.

'What's happened here? Who is responsible for this? What do you know about it?'

'Ah,' said Abraham, 'well, when you were out a terrible quarrel broke out among the statues and the biggest statue got so angry about it that he got a hammer and broke all the others up.'

Terah gazed dumbfounded at his son.

'The biggest statue broke the others up? You expect me to believe rubbish like that? How could a statue do that – it has no power!'

'True,' said Abraham. 'Why then do you worship a statue and sell them to other people to worship? How can any man worship something which has no power?'

For a very long moment there was silence. Then Terah looked for a long time at Abraham.

'Son,' he said, 'sometimes we need to learn a lesson. You have taught me one today.'

Information for the teacher

1 A *midrash* is a traditional story which highlights characters and events to reinforce scriptural teachings. This morning's story is a *midrash*. Abraham is the Father of the Jewish Nation and there are several such stories about him. Other stories about Abraham can be found in the Torah and in the Old Testament. (Genesis 22 is the story of Abraham and Isaac his son.)

   The Torah is written in Hebrew. The Hebrew language has no vowels in it and is read from left to right.
2 This story could be told in either February or March, to coincide with the Jewish festival of Purim. This festival celebrates an event of over two thousand years ago when Haman, an official in the royal court of Persia, wanted to exterminate all the Jews in Persia. He arranged for lots to be cast to decide how this should be done. (The word for 'lots' is 'purim'.) However, Esther, the Jewish queen of the Persian King Ahasuerus, found out that the plot would start by the hanging of her uncle Mordecai. She warned the king in time and Haman was hanged. (Bible reference: Book of Esther)

   Purim has been celebrated joyfully ever since and every time Haman's name is mentioned in the synagogue on this date it is greeted with rude noises. Many of the latter are made with a grogger, which is a noisy rattle.
3 A useful address for Jewish affairs is: Jewish Education Bureau, 8 Westcombe Avenue, Leeds L58 2BS.

Hymn suggestion

Come and Praise Vol 2 'And ev'ryone beneath the vine' No 149

Prayer

Let us give thanks this morning that we are free to come to school, have teachers to help us learn, have the chance to celebrate things and can talk and sing and pray together.

National Curriculum cross-curricular reference

Both the assembly story, and the story which is the basis of Purim celebrations, are very good vehicles for drama. The Purim story is also good for devising suitable improvised music to highlight its development from plotting, through fear, threat and revelation to celebration.

The idea of 'a child's point of view' is also a good one for promoting discussions from which written personal opinions could be developed.

History and RE could be well served by researching the original events concerning the characters in both stories.

44 *Fame*

Introduction

When we are young we sometimes dream that we will be famous one day. But being a famous person can have its worries too . . .

Story

Nellie Melba tore open the envelope and read the words which were written on the sheet of paper inside it.

The letter was dated March, 1893, and it said, 'Twenty minutes after the curtain rises and you make your first appearance on stage, you will be dead.'

Now, you might think Nellie had done something dreadful to deserve this threat, but you would be wrong. In 1893 Nellie Melba was probably the most famous singer in the world and the letter was sent to her by a music lover in Milan, in Italy, because he was annoyed that she had won her fame in other cities before coming to sing in Milan!

The worst thing that happened when she finally began to sing in the Milan Opera House, however, was that a man tried to throw a bunch of flowers to her.

Nellie's fame was hard-earned and she had no easy start to life. She spent her childhood in Australia where her father was an unsuccessful goldminer. She hated school and stayed away whenever she could – but she loved music and singing.

When she was six years old she appeared in her first concert in Melbourne. She sang an old Scottish song called 'Comin' Through the Rye' and this made her determined that more than anything in life she wanted to be a singer.

Saving desperately hard, she eventually had enough money to catch a ship to Paris where she hoped to take singing lessons. Once she got there she made an appointment with a famous singing teacher called Madame Marchesi.

Madame Marchesi looked at the keen Australian girl and decided that she had better prepare her for disappointment.

'Now look here, young lady,' she said. 'I hardly take anybody for singing lessons because they're just not good enough. In fact, you could say I've turned down more people than there are sheep in Australia, so you can't say I haven't warned you. Now, sing.'

When Nellie began to sing, however, Madame Marchesi was enthralled. The young singer had hardly finished before the teacher leaped to her feet to say, 'You're going to be a star!'

For years after that Nellie sang in the great cities of the world giving pleasure to thousands of people. No matter how famous or how busy she became, she always had time for little kindnesses to ordinary people.

In 1894 she was singing in London. She so enjoyed the food in the hotel in which she was staying that she gave the chef two very expensive, and hard-to-get, tickets for one of her shows.

'That's fantastic,' said the chef. 'Such kindness deserves a special Thank You. I'm going to make up a new sweet and call it after you, madame.'

The chef disappeared into the kitchen. There he peeled some peaches and put them in a vanilla sauce. Next he lay the peaches on a layer of vanilla ice cream and then covered the whole thing with a raspberry sauce.

Now, if you ever ask for a Peach Melba, you will know how it got its name.

Information for the teacher

1 The calendar anniversary for this story was the March occasion of
the Milanese threats. These were taken very seriously at the time
and the theatre was packed with both uniformed and plain-clothed
policemen.

   Nellie Melba was born Nellie Mitchell. Other significant dates in
her life were: her birth in May 1861 in Melbourne, Australia; her
death in the same place in 1930.

2 There are several themes which can be drawn from this story. Two
are: the determination which is needed to succeed; and the
pleasure and enjoyment we get from seeing and hearing a brilliant
artist perform.

   There is a most appropriate Bible reference here:

   'I know that there is nothing good for a man except to be happy
and live the best life he can while he is alive. Moreover, that a man
should eat and drink and enjoy himself, in return for all his
labours, is a gift of God. A merry heart keeps a man alive, and joy
lengthens the span of his days.' (Ecclesiasticus 30, 21–22)

   For those who want to follow this up with an appropriate
'linking' Biblical story, 2 Samuel 6, 12–22, tells of the celebrations
when the Ark of the Covenant was brought to the city of
Jerusalem.

Hymn suggestion

Come and Praise Vol 2 'Let the world rejoice together' No 148

Prayer

Let us give thanks this morning for all those who bring so much
pleasure to our lives by their skill and talent in entertaining us. Let us
give thanks for singers, actors and actresses, artists, writers and
sportsmen and women. Amen.

National Curriculum cross-curricular reference

There is plenty of scope for linking Music with this story. As Nellie
Melba was an opera singer, one or two short and carefully chosen
pieces of opera music might be played to the children.

Her story also provides for dramatic opportunities. Locating European cities with famous opera houses (Paris, Vienna, Milan, etc) would be an interesting geographical exercise when compared with their distances from Australia.

45 Thanks, driver!

Introduction

Sometimes in our day-to-day lives something dangerous happens. If it does we should hope that there is somebody around like John Robson. This is his story.

Story

Thursday, March 15th, was just like another normal working day. John Robson left his home in Bruce Castle Road, Tottenham, and went off to work – to drive an Underground train in London's hustle and bustle.

By the afternoon he was driving a train along the Piccadilly line in the rush hour. This meant that the carriages on his train were packed full with seven hundred people.

'You'd wonder where all these people came from,' thought John to himself, as he eased down the speed of his train to stop at a red light in a tunnel at King's Cross. 'Still, I'll soon be finished and off home for my tea.'

John's thoughts stopped abruptly, his eyes opened wide and the hair on the back of his neck began to prickle with fright. Round a bend in front of him, another train had suddenly appeared. Its headlights shone in his eyes and the train was heading straight for him.

'Oh no!' gasped John. A terrible crash seemed absolutely certain.

Then John leapt into action. Flinging back his driver's door, he reached out and grabbed two wires which ran along the side of the Underground tunnel. Brushing the dust off them and ignoring the mild shock the wires were sending through his hands, he slowly brought the two ends of the wires together.

'Work, please work!' begged John as he held the wires together.

Like a charging monster, the oncoming train raced towards him. Its lights glistened like angry eyes as it rocked and swayed in the noisy tunnel. Then, painfully slowly, it began to lose speed. John held his breath as the train got nearer, and nearer, and then slowed to a stop just a few yards in front of his own train.

John slumped down in his seat and, for a moment, put his head in his hands to calm himself. Another few seconds and over a thousand people would have been involved in a terrible accident.

Later, London Transport praised Mr Robson's brave, quick-thinking action. One of their officers said, 'By using the low-voltage wires as he did, Mr Robson switched off the current from the track and turned on the tunnel's emergency lighting. There's no doubt he was a hero and there are plenty of people to say, "Thanks, driver".'

Information for the teacher

1 This incident took place on 15th March 1990. Special signals to prevent this sort of thing happening had been installed in many areas following recommendations made in 1988. A major inquiry followed this incident.

   The low-voltage line-side wires are specially designed to switch the current from the track and light up the tunnel. All the Underground train drivers are taught how to use these low-voltage wires to cut off the power.
2 A useful address in connection with this story is: Public Relations Officer, London Transport Executive, 55 Broadway, Westminster, London SW1H 0BB. (This organisation prefers teachers to write direct for information, material, folder maps of rail services, etc.)
3 This story could be one of a series where ordinary people perform extraordinary actions which save lives. Such a series can be constantly kept up-to-date and fresh by stockpiling newspaper stories.

Hymn suggestion

Come and Praise Vol 1 'He who would valiant be' No 44

Prayer

Dear God,
Let us give thanks this morning for ordinary people who, so often, by their quick thinking, bravery and determination, save the lives of others. Thank you for your guidance. Amen.

National Curriculum cross-curricular reference

There are a lot of Maths possibilities in examining railway timetables, and 'stopping time' is a useful theme for Science, starting with simple practical work using model cars and varied gradients.

Another aspect of Science which could be involved here is the making, and breaking, of simple electrical circuits. Locating safety measures in various places (for instance, the low-voltage wires in Underground tunnels) could provide scope for Technology.

46   The lost sheep

Introduction

None of us likes to lose anything. In this morning's story something is lost – and then found again. It is a story to make us think.

Story

Benjamin was a shepherd. Whatever the weather, his long cloak protected him against sun, wind and rain. His bag of food was always well filled because he was not sure when he could refill it. With bread, cheese, olives and raisins bouncing against his hip, and money and small stones in the girdle round his waist, Benjamin quite happily trudged the lonely miles behind his sheep.

'Soon be time for a rest,' he said to himself as the sunset turned the sky into a brilliant red. As he spoke, his fingers felt the reed pipes which he played after eating his supper, before going to sleep.

Ahead the shepherd saw the sheepfold into which he would gather his flock for the night. Here, surrounded by brick walls and with himself sleeping in the doorway, his sheep would be safe from snakes, wolves and any other kind of prowler.

'Come on, my beauties,' said Benjamin quietly. 'In we go.'

Matching his actions with his words, the shepherd poked and prodded his sheep to guide them into the safety of the sheepfold. As he did so he counted each one as it passed through the small entranceway.

Knowing that he had exactly one hundred sheep, Benjamin was

disturbed when ninety-nine had passed into the sheepfold – and there were no others to be seen.

'Oh no,' muttered Benjamin. 'One of them must have got lost on that rocky path near the mountains.'

Putting rocks across the entrance to keep the sheep in, Benjamin then turned and began the long walk back to where the path had been flanked by rock-strewn cracks and crevices. All the while he whistled softly through his teeth, partly to make the lost sheep feel better. He knew that alone, and in danger from its enemies, it would be nervous and afraid.

With darkness falling, his feet ached as he reclimbed the rocky footpath, looking on either side as he did so. Half an hour passed before he saw a sudden movement in a crevice off to the right of the path. It was the missing sheep, terrified and motionless.

Soothingly, Benjamin called to it as he stretched his hand into the crevice. Then, with his long staff, he helped it back up onto the path. The sheep was still shaking with fear and weakness. Bending down, Benjamin took its forelegs in one hand and its hindlegs in the other. With a mighty lift he swung it astride his shoulders and began the long walk back to the sheepfold.

Weary but satisfied, Benjamin began to whistle again – pausing only to mutter to himself, 'Ninety-nine, one hundred – now they're *all* safe again.'

Information for the teacher

1 The text refers to the shepherd's girdle containing 'money and small stones'. The small stones were thrown to attract the sheep's attention. The shepherd's reed pipes and the rain's horn were Israel's earliest musical instruments.

   Sheepfolds were stone enclosures and shepherds often slept across the entrance when the sheep were all safely inside for the night.

2 The good shepherd is obviously a symbolic Biblical figure. His characteristics include faithfulness, diligence, tenderness and the readiness to risk his own life to look after his charges. There are many Bible references extolling such virtues: John 10, 11; Ezekiel 34, 11–16; Psalm 78, 70–72.

3 References for this particular story are Matthew 18, 11–14; Luke 15, 4–7.

4 From a calendar point of view this story could be used to lead up to assembly and/or RE work on Easter.

Hymn suggestion

Come and Praise Vol 1 'The Lord's my shepherd' No 56

Prayer

Dear God,
Help us to understand the meaning of this morning's story. Teach us to remember that every single person is important.

Help us to remember that everyone has hopes, worries, fears, joys and disappointments, just as we do. Amen.

National Curriculum cross-curricular reference

Science and Geography could be interwoven with research into sheep, their physical needs and areas of the world which are particularly suited to their rearing. The history of shepherds is another theme which could be pursued and the construction of sheepfolds and caves could incorporate Technology.

Some experimentation in Music and Technology could be done in devising and testing 'reed pipes' – straws, etc.

47   The Ethel Langton story

Introduction

Sometimes, if we are caught in an unexpected situation, we have to act in a way which requires all our courage and determination. Listen to Ethel Langton's story.

Story

Ethel Langton was fifteen years old and she was the daughter of a lighthouse keeper. Mr Langton's lighthouse was near the Isle of Wight, a quarter of a mile out to sea. In March 1926 this lighthouse overlooked one of the busiest stretches of water in the world. Huge liners, tankers, tugs and merchant ships sailed daily by, to and from Southampton.

Without the St Helen's light shining at night, hundreds of seamen's lives would have been at risk. The light itself was an oil burner. Every day the wick had to be trimmed and the oil filled up. The light was situated on top of a twenty-foot tower and could only be reached by climbing an outside steel ladder. Doing this was very dangerous in bad weather.

'Right, my love,' said Mr Langton to his daughter on Saturday, 20th March 1926. 'Your mum and I are going ashore to do the week's shopping. We'll see you and Badge at dinner time.'

'OK, Dad,' replied Ethel, looking at the calm sea and scratching Badge's ear. Badge was the family dog.

Used to the routine, Ethel read for a while after her parents had gone. After a short time she was aware that the waves were being whipped up by an ever-increasing wind.

'Hope they get back before the storm starts, Badge,' she said to the dog. 'Otherwise they'll have a rough trip.'

Ethel's hopes were dashed when the storm worsened with sudden and savage ferocity. Now the waves were pounding the beach, spume filled the air and the wind howled terrifyingly. The hours of daylight slipped away frighteningly quickly and Ethel realised that her parents could never make it back in these conditions.

'There's nothing else for it, Badge,' she said. 'I'll have to climb up and see to the light. But first let's have something to eat.'

Then came another unpleasant surprise. The only food she could find was half a loaf of bread and a few spoonfuls of sugar. She shared this with Badge and then braced herself to deal with the light.

As she opened the door the savage wind almost blew her over. Determinedly, she got down and crawled over to the ladder attached to the light tower. Getting her foot on the bottom rung, she began the terrifying climb. Halfway up her scarf was torn from her neck and disappeared into the dusk. When she was almost at the top, one of her feet was blown off a rung and for a few dizzying seconds she hung on only by her hands.

Finally she reached the light. Checking it out, she got it lit before darkness fell, and then began the perilous descent.

Through the night, Ethel made several journeys to see that the light was working properly. Hardly daring to sleep for more than a few minutes at a time, soaking wet and desperately hungry, she felt sure the storm would soon die down.

'When it does,' she said to Badge, 'Mum and Dad will be back in a flash – and won't I be glad!'

With the coming of dawn she fell into an exhausted sleep in an armchair. She was awakened by Badge nuzzling her.

'Oh, Badge,' she said, 'what's the weather like?'

The roar of the wind and the crashing of the waves soon told her. 'We could be in for another busy night,' thought Ethel. 'I'd better get up and prepare the light.'

This time, when she reached the light, Ethel had to trim the wick, fill it up with oil and wind the mechanism. This took her well over an hour – but the light was now ready to be lit when darkness fell.

Back indoors Ethel thought longingly of a hot meal and she and Badge lay tightly together to try and keep warm. The next day passed in another roaring frenzy, to be followed by several more terrifying climbs up the ladder during the night.

By the next morning Ethel was completely exhausted. She was so cold, tired and hungry that she could hardly stand. 'But I may have to do more than that,' she thought. 'Maybe I'll have to keep the light going for another night!'

As the day went on, however, the storm began to abate gradually and in late afternoon she saw a lifeboat put out from the shore. Her parents were on board and her ordeal was soon over.

That was not the end of the story, however. Ethel's courage was described in all the newspapers and, at fifteen, she became the youngest person ever to receive the Lloyd's Medal for Meritorious Service.

Information for the teacher

1 This storm in March 1926 was described at the time as being the 'worst in living memory' for those parts.
2 A useful comparison could be made between facilities available in 1926 and those available now. Significant items might be things like helicopters, frozen food in deep freezers, etc.

Hymn suggestion

Come and Praise Vol 1 'He who would valiant be' No 44

Prayer

Let us bow our heads and give thanks to those people who, all over the world and every day, show courage in helping their fellows. Let us all learn from their determination and unselfishness.

National Curriculum cross-curricular reference

The history of lighthouses is a far-reaching topic, as is their geographical location round the British Isles and elsewhere in the world. Some Science and Technology possibilities are obvious in practical work making models of lighting circuits.

48 All change

Introduction

Have you ever thought that you would like to be bigger . . . or smaller . . . or fatter . . . or thinner? George was a carpenter and he thought he would like to be something else.

Story

George was a carpenter, and a good one. With his clever hands and his trusty tools he produced beautiful tables, chairs, bookcases and wardrobes.

'But I'm fed up with it,' he thought one day to himself. 'All day turning pieces of wood into furniture, selling them, starting all over again. I bet other jobs are easier and more enjoyable than mine.'

On his way to work every day George passed a painter's studio. The very next morning he called in.

'Errol, my friend,' said George to the artist. 'I'm fed up with being a carpenter. I want to be an artist. Will you teach me?'

Errol the artist looked at George for a long time. Then he said, 'Come with me.'

The two men went into a back room. Leaning against a wall was a large picture.

'How long do you think it took me to do that?' asked Errol.

'I've no idea,' replied George.

'Six months – and I still can't get it right.'

'You mean – it can take you six months to do one picture?' gasped the incredulous George.

'Oh yes,' replied Errol. 'And remember, if no one wants to buy your pictures – life gets very hard.'

'Hmm,' muttered George and, rather sheepishly, he left the studio.

As he continued on his way to work he heard the sound of beautiful piano music coming from a cottage. He stopped and went to the door.

' 'Morning Mrs Masefield. I heard you playing the piano. It was wonderful. Can you teach me to play like that?'

'I don't know, George,' said Mrs Masefield. 'Have you got supple fingers and a good sense of rhythm?'

'Most definitely,' replied George, thinking of how his fingers seemed to have minds of their own when he was carving wood.

And are you prepared to practise for six hours a day?'

'Six hours . . . six hours – *practising*?'

'Yes, if you want to reach this standard.'

'Oh,' muttered George. 'Oh.' And he went on his way.

'These jobs are no good,' he thought to himself. 'I need one that's out in the open air – with no worries.'

At that moment he was passing Simpson Hall, a beautiful old mansion with a huge and magnificent garden, well cared for. Looking down the path he saw Arnold, the head gardener, hard at work on a border.

' 'Morning, Arnold,' said George, wandering down the path.

' 'Morning, George,' replied the gardener.

'Lovely job you've got here,' said George. 'Lovely job, out in the open air, healthy. No pressure, rewarding. Lovely . . .'

At that moment there was the sound of rapidly approaching footsteps. Lord Kilrain, the owner of the hall, was striding briskly towards them.

'Ah, Arnold, when you've done that, fix up the grass tennis court so that we can play on it this afternoon. Oh, and then make a start putting the marquee up. We've got a hundred and fifty guests coming to the party. And by the way, that lawnmower needs some attention . . .'

Hoping that he wouldn't be noticed, George slipped away as quietly as he could. Suddenly being a carpenter didn't seem such a bad job after all.

Information for the teacher

1 A useful calendar link for this story is 19th March, which is St Joseph's feast day. As a carpenter, Joseph always enjoyed a prominent place in the performances of mystery plays in the Middle Ages. These were usually presented by craftsmen's guilds.

2 A useful folk tale to link with this story is the one about the

shoemaker by La Fontaine. A shoemaker was very happy in his work until he was given a present by a rich neighbour. He became obsessed with guarding, hiding and counting the gold. He couldn't concentrate on his shoemaking and became very unhappy.

Realising what was wrong, he gave the gold back to his neighbour and became a contented worker again.

Hymn suggestion

Come and Praise Vol 2 ' 'Tis the gift to be simple' No 97

Prayer

Dear God,
Let us pray this morning for those people who work with their hands. Help us to show our appreciation for what they do and give them contentment and satisfaction in their work. Amen.

National Curriculum cross-curricular reference

'Trades and professions' is a subject which could give rise to a lot of research in History. Technology and Science could embrace skilled workers and their tools, and include some practical activities. Themes like 'satisfaction and contentment' could provoke useful discussion, especially with upper juniors.

49 Hero Wong

Introduction

We often hear stories of dogs coming to the rescue of their masters or mistresses. Cats, however, are another matter – or are they?

Story

'Oh, she'll be all right on the lawn for a minute or two.' So said Mrs Viviers as she looked out into the sunshine and saw her daughter Wanda, playing happily with her toys. It was a beautiful day and everything was calm and peaceful in the Johannesburg street where the Viviers lived.

'Right,' replied Mr Viviers. 'It will only take us a few minutes to rearrange this furniture. Then we'll go out on the lawn too and have our tea.'

Meanwhile, four-year-old Wanda was quite happy as she stepped in and out of her paddling pool, singing as she did so. She could hear her mum and dad talking in the house and somewhere in the distance a radio played softly. Then, suddenly, she heard a new and strange noise. It was a sort of slithering . . .

'I wonder what that can be?' thought Wanda to herself. Then she turned – and felt a chill of absolute terror run right through her.

Sliding towards her over the lawn was a huge snake. Its five-foot-long body hissed over the grass and its hooded head swayed horribly towards her.

Wanda screamed – but another wild, screeching noise was even louder. Suddenly, there was a flash of hurling, spitting fur and Wong, Wanda's Siamese cat, threw himself in front of her. As the snake's head swayed threateningly, Wong scratched defensively at the long body. For what seemed a lifetime the air was alive with hissing and howling as again and again the little cat attacked the dangerous invader.

By now Mr and Mrs Viviers had heard the noise and were racing down the lawn. In her fear, Wanda had not moved, and Wong was still darting and leaping to protect her. Suddenly the snake had had enough. Sliding away as quickly as it had arrived, it was chased all the way by the cat.

Mrs Viviers had now reached her daughter and swept Wanda up into her arms. 'Are you all right? Wanda! Speak to me!'

'All right, all right, Mummy,' gasped the little girl.

'Thanks to Wong!' murmured Mr Viviers, bending down to stroke the panting, trembling little Siamese cat.

Information for the teacher

1 Many of the children will be aware that very few animals are prepared to attack a snake – the armadillo and the mongoose being two of those who do. For a cat to do so is very rare – particularly in this instance when the creature was a five-foot-long Ringhalls snake.

2 Not surprisingly, this story appeared in newspapers throughout the world and in London the PDSA awarded Wong a silver medal for his life-saving bravery.

3 As a calendar reference, 20th March is one possibility. This is St

Cuthbert's Day – among his many other accomplishments, Cuthbert was supposed to have a remarkable affinity with animals.

On another 'animal' theme, 17th March was considered in mediaeval times to be the day on which Noah entered the Ark.

Hymn suggestion

Come and Praise Vol 2 'All the animals' No 80

Prayer

Let us think this morning about the word 'Thanks'. Do we say it as often as we should? Do we think enough about all the people to whom we should be grateful for looking after us and helping us in our daily lives?

Let us spend a quiet minute thinking about all that we should be thankful for.

National Curriculum cross-curricular reference

Geography could be linked to locating Johannesburg and finding out some of its characteristics. Science could be involved in doing some research on snakes and their habits.

The story could lead to plenty of English work, too – the children could discuss characteristics of their own pets. Some might have first-hand examples of 'pet bravery', and this could certainly be followed by stories collected from newspapers, books, and magazines. There is also much scope for children's own creative writing within this theme.

50 What is your opinion?

Introduction

Sometimes people's cruelty to animals is almost unbelievable – as this morning's story shows.

Story

'I've got to get help for these poor creatures – I just *must*.'

The man who thought these words to himself was a lorry driver. On one of his latest jobs he had been asked to drive a truckload of forty Shetland ponies across the border of Northern Ireland, towards Dublin in the south. He had been absolutely appalled at the condition they were in. This is their story.

The ponies were sold at an auction in the Shetlands. Then they were taken by boat from the Shetlands to Northern Ireland. Later they were crammed into the lorry which took them on to southern Ireland. When they reached Dublin they were to be sold at Smithfield Market.

The ponies' journey from the Shetlands to Dublin took three weeks. During all this time they had hardly any food or water and no thought was given to their travelling conditions.

When the lorry driver had delivered them to the market in Dublin, he reported the ponies' terrible condition. A vet was rushed to the scene. He was horrified at what he found. Only nine of the ponies were left at the market and all of these were in a distressed state. They had pus running from their eyes and noses and all of them had a disease called ringworm. Some of them could hardly stand, they were so weak.

'Well, at least I know where these nine will be properly looked after and given a good home,' said the vet.

He contacted Redwings Horse Sanctuary, near Norwich, and made arrangements for the ponies to be taken there. The good news is that all nine ponies made a good recovery in the caring atmosphere of Redwings.

But what of the other ponies, who had been crammed in – forty to the truck? Nobody knows their fate but there have been reports of such ponies being sold cheaply and ridden until they drop dead of exhaustion or illness.

How can some human beings behave so cruelly?

(The information for this story comes from a Redwings newsletter.)

Information for the teacher

1 Redwings Horse Sanctuary (Hill Top Farm, Hall Lane, Frettenham, nr. Norwich, NR12 7LT, telephone 0603 737432) organises school visits and anyone interested should contact the School Visits Department at the above address. The sanctuary looks after 1,200 horses and there are schemes like 'adopt a pony or donkey' which cost just £6 per year.

   The sanctuary, via managers, vets and welfare staff, are anxious to help educate children in the 'battle to prevent unnecessary suffering'. There is also a newsletter available from the same address.

2 A useful calendar and literary link here is with *Black Beauty*. There are obvious connections between the two stories, and the author, Anna Sewell, was born on 30th March 1820.

Hymn suggestion

Come and Praise Vol 1 'All the animals' No 80

Prayer

Let us pray this morning for all animals everywhere who are suffering at the hands of human beings.

Let us remember that, though they have no words with which to complain, they still feel pain and distress.

Let us pray for the guidance of those people who cause animals to be hurt. Amen.

National Curriculum cross-curricular reference

The most obvious link here is with Science: basic needs of animals; evidence of good and bad health; characteristics of horses. From a History viewpoint the horse as a helpmate to humans could be examined in more detail.

51 *I need some help*

Introduction

It is hard to imagine a more frightening situation than the one in which John found himself. When you listen to John's story, I'm sure you'll agree!

Story

The small plane droned peacefully through the sky above Wales. In the distance Les Rhoades, the pilot, and John Anderson, his passenger, could see the distant outline of Cardiff airport.

'Soon be there now,' said Les.

'Smashing little plane, this,' answered John, looking out along the wing of the Rally Minerva aircraft.

'Yes, it's . . .' Suddenly, Les gave a choking noise and slumped forward in his seat.

'Les? *Les!*'

John reached across and shook the pilot without success. Les was deeply unconscious, and the plane began to rock uncertainly.

'What shall I do?' gasped John aloud. 'I've never even *touched* the controls of a plane before.'

Gritting his teeth and forcing himself to stay calm, John radioed the Air Traffic Controller at Cardiff airport with an emergency Mayday call.

'I need some help,' he said as calmly as he could, and then explained the situation.

On the ground the controller reacted quickly to the emergency. 'How can we get him down?'

'What's the best thing to do?'

'What about contacting Robert? He's airborne at the moment.'

Robert was flying instructor Robert Legg who was flying nearby with a pupil in his Piper Warrior. He was quickly contacted by radio.

'OK,' replied Robert, 'I understand. I'll call him on my radio.'

So began a nerve-racking time. Robert called John on the radio and, bit by bit, told him what to do with his hands and feet to keep the plane flying.

'From what you tell me, you've got plenty of fuel,' said Robert. 'All we're going to do at the moment is give you a bit of practice.'

'OK,' answered John. 'I've never done anything like this before.'

So, in the skies above the airport, the two planes began circling as John tried to get used to the controls.

'You're doing absolutely great,' said Robert encouragingly. 'I think we're about ready to land now.'

'If you think so,' answered John.

Inch by inch the Rally Minerva dropped as Robert's calm voice told John exactly what to do. Slowly it was lined up with the runway and began to sink even lower.

Out of the corner of his eye John could see things flashing past as he listened to the voice in his ear and struggled to keep the plane on an even keel. Then, with a *clunck*, he felt the wheels touch the ground.

Still concentrating for all he was worth, he eased back the speed and the plane gradually rolled to a stop. He was back on the ground – and safe!

Information for the teacher

1 This incident took place on 31st March 1992. Les Rhoades, a businessman, was twenty-three-year-old John Anderson's father-in-law. Sadly, Mr Rhoades had suffered a heart attack and was dead on arrival at Llandough Hospital, Cardiff.

Speaking of the incident afterwards, Robert Legg said of John: 'He made a perfect landing. He did marvellously well.'

2 There are several Bible references which are appropriate to this story:

'One man wins success by his words; another gets his due reward by the work of his hands.' (Proverbs 12, 14)

'Prepare yourself for testing, Set a straight course, be resolute, Do not lose your head in time of disaster.' (Ecclesiasticus 2, 1–2)

'Woe to faint hearts and nerveless hands.' (Ecclesiasticus 2, 12)

Hymn suggestion

Come and Praise Vol 1 'He who would valiant be' No 44

Prayer

Dear God,

We pray that we may be given the skill, courage and resourcefulness to deal with difficulties in our lives. We also give thanks for those many people who are always ready to help us. Amen.

National Curriculum cross-curricular reference

Science could be very much involved in researching and studying flight. This could also embrace Technology in both preparatory and practical work.

English could be involved with the children discussing and writing about situations within their own experience when they have been worried or frightened by unusual circumstances.

April

52 *A good joke*

Introduction

If we enjoy a joke with our friends then laughing together is fun. To laugh *with* somebody is good, to laugh *at* somebody can often be cruel.

Today's story is about a good April Fools' Day joke which everybody enjoyed.

Story

Most of us enjoy watching television – particularly when programmes make us laugh. Some years ago the producers of a TV programme called *Panorama* decided that they would play a joke on the whole of Britain.

'We've got a programme due to go out on April 1st,' said the chief producer. 'We're going to use it for a great joke. Now, this is what we are going to do . . .'

After he had finished explaining, writers, camera operators and all the other programme staff prepared themselves for spending a few days in Switzerland. They were very excited about the idea.

'What a joke! Do you think anybody will believe it?'

'I think they will if we do it well enough.'

'So it'll have to be well done.'

'I can't wait to see the finished programme.'

Soon all the programme's staff arrived in Switzerland. Once there, they went to a little village near Lake Lugano. Their next job was to unpack some special material they had brought with them – this was over twenty tons of cooked spaghetti!

Once they had unpacked the spaghetti they got a number of ladders. Climbing these, they began to hang the spaghetti from the branches of a group of trees in the village. Soon the trees were completely covered with spaghetti draped all over them. Now it was time for the next step!

'Now we've got to get the Swiss people living in the village to help us,' explained the chief producer. 'We'll get them all to wear farm workers' clothes and they can collect the spaghetti from the trees and pack it in large baskets. While they're doing this the cameras will shoot them from lots of angles. Then the writers will write the script to go with the film.'

Soon everyone was having fun as the 'spaghetti harvest' was collected in. Then, when all the films had been successfully taken, the programme staff packed up and returned to England.

It soon came round to April 1st and all over Britain people switched their television sets on to watch *Panorama*.

'Good evening, ladies and gentlemen,' said a voice, as the pictures on the screen showed the Swiss countryside flashing by.

'Today we are visiting a small village in Switzerland where the local people grow an unusual crop. We will watch them harvesting their produce.'

So the words went on, and as they did the pictures showed the trees, heavy with their 'spaghetti crop'. Then there were lots more pictures of the people harvesting the crop.

The joke was a great success. Millions of people, realising the date, and watching spaghetti 'growing' on trees, had a really good laugh at the programme. A few didn't realise it was a joke and rang up the BBC to ask where they could buy spaghetti trees!

Information for the teacher

1 The theme of 'laughing with' rather than 'laughing at' (in the sense of derision, etc) is a very important one with young children and can stand a fair amount of repetition. This April 1st story provides a starting point for its development via further discussion.

2 The origin of April Fools' Day is obscure. Indeed, *Poor Robin's Almanac* of 1760 said:

> The First of April, some do say
> Is set apart for All Fools' Day;
> But why the people call it so,
> Not I, nor they themselves, do know.

One suggestion had been that it is the aftermath of a festival celebrating the Celtic god of Mirth; another is that it was traditionally a day of frivolity to celebrate the end of winter and the coming of spring.

This is a time of year when 'fooling' goes on not only in English-speaking countries and Europe, but also in India when the great spring festival of Holi involves a lot of fun with throwing coloured water and powder.

Hymn suggestion

Come and Praise Vol 2 'You shall go out with joy' No 98

Prayer

This is an occasion for using a well-known and very good prayer. It is the anonymous offering found in Chester cathedral:

> Give me a good digestion, Lord,
> And always something to digest;
> Give me a healthy body, Lord,
> With sense to keep it at its best.
>
> Give me healthy eyes, good Lord,
> To keep the good and pure in sight,
> Which seeing sin is not appalled
> But finds a way to set it right.
>
> Give me a mind that is not bored,
> That does not whimper, whine or sigh;
> Don't let me worry overmuch
> About the fussy thing called I.
>
> Give me a sense of humour, Lord,
> Give me the grace to see a joke,
> To get some happiness from life
> And pass it on to other folk.

National Curriculum cross-curricular reference

The story in the text, and other April Fool jokes (of which the children usually know quite a few) provide good discussion points. Creative and descriptive writing and drama could also be drawn from these starters.

'Fun' music could be improvised and listened to. Recordings for listening could range from Haydn's *Toy Symphony* to the many and varied humorous songs which have appeared over the years – Flanders and Swann's 'Hippopotamus', 'The Laughing Policeman', Charlie Drake's 'My Boomerang Won't Come Back', etc.

53   *The second chance*

Introduction

I expect most of you have heard an adult say at some time: 'Oh, I wish I had worked harder at school.' This morning's story makes us think about that.

Story

The boy didn't like school. He didn't work very hard there and, when he got the chance, he stayed away. So he fell further and further behind in his work. He didn't mind though, it didn't matter – he was going to be a famous singer.

In the big city where he lived there was a great opera house. Most of the world's most famous singers performed there. Whenever the boy got the chance he went to the opera house. Day after day, week after week, he could be seen there.

The musicians and singers got used to seeing him – and talking to him.

'Why do you hang around here, boy?'

'I'm going to be a great opera singer.'

'Have you had any training?'

'No.'

'You're wasting your time then – you'll never make it.'

But the boy kept coming. One day the singers and musicians got together.

'Perhaps this lad's a genius.'

'He's certainly determined.'

'Let's give him a chance.'

So one day when the boy arrived at the opera house the musicians were waiting for him.

'Come on,' they said, 'we've set aside ten minutes to hear you sing.'

The boy wasn't at all nervous. After all, a singer was what he was going to be.

The musicians got ready. The boy began to sing. For a minute or two there was absolute silence. Then, someone began to laugh. Within seconds all the singers and musicians were roaring with laughter. The boy was *awful* – the very worst singer any of them had heard.

One of the ladies in the group, however, felt sorry for him. 'Come on,' she said, 'you'll never make a singer because you haven't got the voice for it. But you must be good at something – and we've still got five minutes left. What else can you do?'

'Well,' said the disappointed boy, 'people say I'm good at telling stories.' And he began to tell one.

Soon there was again silence, but it was not followed by laughter. The boy's story was marvellous, his audience were entranced. When he'd finished they burst into applause.

'That was wonderful,' said the lady. 'Write that story down. I think the king should know about your talent.'

So, excitedly, the boy went home – to disappointment and frustration. Because he had paid no attention at school he couldn't write very well and his spelling was very bad indeed. Eventually, after hours of work, he got the story written and took it to the lady.

When the king read the story he stroked his chin and then spoke to all the people waiting expectantly round him. 'The story is great,' he said, 'but the writing and spelling are dreadful. Send this fellow back to school so he can learn to do these things properly and send the bill to me. Then I want to see his next story.'

So the boy went back to school and this time he worked hard and paid attention. After some time he found he could not only tell stories well, but write them well too. The king was impressed and asked for more and more stories. Other people did too. Soon the stories were being published in books. People all over the boy's country were reading them. Soon they were translated into other languages and eventually the whole world was enjoying them – it still is. Oh yes – the boy's name, if you haven't already guessed it, was Hans Andersen.

Information for the teacher

1 Hans Christian Andersen was born on 2nd April 1805 in Odense, Denmark. The son of a poor shoemaker, he sought to start his singing career at the Copenhagen Opera House. The king who paid for his schooling was Frederick IV – although just when this was is not altogether clear.

   Andersen died in 1875 having already become world famous. 'The Emperor's New Clothes' is arguably his most famous story, and certainly one which primary school children enjoy.

Hymn suggestion

Come and Praise Vol 1 'The best gift' No 59

Prayer

First of all this morning we can listen to some words from the Bible: 'Let us now sing the praises of famous men.' (Ecclesiasticus 44)

Let us give thanks for those people who write stories and books which give us so much pleasure.

Let us give thanks for all those people whose special talents make our lives so much more interesting and enjoyable. Amen.

National Curriculum cross-curricular reference

English is the most obvious link here, with opportunities to involve the children in listening, telling and writing stories, discussion, and drama. 'Telling and writing for an audience' is a theme which might be particularly appropriate.

54   Is that really what you want?

Introduction

You might know somebody who never seems to be content. 'I wish I had that . . . I wish I could go there . . . I wish I was . . .' This morning's story is a particularly good one for discontented people to listen to.

Story

Many years ago two kings lived near each other on islands in the Pacific Ocean. King Tuwara was a crafty fellow who was always trying to get the best for himself and his subjects. King Wa-Kulikuli was foolish and envious and always thought other people had more and better things than himself.

Now it so happened that Wa-Kulikuli came one day to visit the island which Tuwara ruled. He had never been there before and he was amazed to see a huge curtain hanging outside Tuwara's house.

'That's a beautiful curtain. I haven't got any like that. Can I have it?' blurted out Wa-Kulikuli.

Tuwara smiled and said, 'Oh no, I'm terribly sorry.'

The curtain was actually to keep mosquitoes from getting into Tuwara's house and biting everybody. Tuwara, however, was rather ashamed that his island had mosquitoes when he knew that there were none on Wa-Kulikuli's island. 'We keep that cloth up because it looks beautiful and it keeps out any cold winds which might blow,' went on Tuwara.

So the two kings went into the house and, as happens on the islands, darkness fell very quickly. As it did so the buzzing of mosquitoes began on the other side of the curtain.

Because there were no mosquitoes on his island Wa-Kulikuli didn't know what they were so he said to Tuwara, 'What's that noise?'

'Ah,' said Tuwara. 'Those are my friends. They come to sing me to sleep when it gets dark.'

'How marvellous,' gasped Wa-Kulikuli. 'I've got nothing like that. Can I see them?'

'No, no, nobody can see them,' said Tuwara. 'They're terribly shy and wouldn't ever want to be seen. That's why we keep the curtain up.'

Not only did Wa-Kulikuli believe this but he got desperately greedy in his foolish way. 'Look, my friend,' he said, 'I'd like those creatures to come and sing me to sleep. Let me buy them from you.'

Tuwara could hardly believe his ears. This silly man actually wanted to buy the mosquitoes which were such a pest to him and all his people! But Tuwara was very crafty – and Wa-Kulikuli had something he wanted.

'Not a chance, old friend,' he said. 'I just couldn't sell them.'

'Now look,' went on Wa-Kulikuli, mopping his brow. 'I really do want those creatures to sing me to sleep. I'll give you anything you like for them.'

Tuwara paused and stroked his chin.

'They are my loyal subjects, you know . . . but . . . perhaps I could arrange to let you have them in exchange for those shellfish you have on your island.'

Everybody around knew that the shellfish on Wa-Kulikuli's island were the best around. But the foolish king had lost all sense of reason – more than anything else he wanted those mosquitoes!

'It's a bargain,' he cried. 'Bring those singing subjects of yours to my island and I'll give you the shellfish.'

Next morning Tuwara captured the mosquitoes in the cave where they lived. He collected them all up in a basket which was so carefully lined that none could escape. Soon the two men were on a boat heading for Wa-Kulikuli's island. When they arrived Tuwara put the basket down on the beach and stood beside it.

'Come on, come on,' cried Wa-Kulikuli impatiently, 'let them out.'

'I couldn't do that,' sighed Tuwara. 'Remember they have been loyal subjects. If they see me here they won't want to leave me.'

So Wa-Kulikuli agreed to collect up all the beautiful-tasting shellfish on his island and put them in Tuwara's boat. When this was done Tuwara said solemnly, 'Let us get completely out of sight before you open the basket, my friend. I certainly wouldn't want any of the mosquitoes to follow me now!'

Well, Wa-Kulikuli could hardly wait to get rid of Tuwara. How he wanted to see these loyal subjects who would come to sing to him every night! The second Tuwara's boat disappeared from sight the foolish king threw the lid of the basket open while all his people looked on.

At once there was an angry buzzing and the mosquitoes swarmed out, biting everyone in sight. From that time onwards nobody could rid the island of them and the people once more sighed and complained at the foolishness of their king.

Meanwhile Tuwara was very happy. He had got rid of his troublesome mosquitoes and obtained some fine food for his people. 'Foolish is the man who wants everything,' he said to his wife.

Information for the teacher

1 This story is adapted from *Tales from the South Pacific Islands* by A Gittins.

2 There are so many folk tales in which greedy, selfish, discontented people get their comeuppance that it is worth making a collection of them. As with this one, they are often ideal for drama. Indeed, for the teacher who wishes it, and has a little more time for preparation, this morning's story could be presented in dramatic form.

3 In dealing with the often self-destructive emotions mentioned above there is an appropriate – and reassuring – Bible reference: 'Each man should examine his own conduct for himself; that he can measure his achievement by comparing himself with himself and not with anyone else.' (Galations 6, 4)

4 A useful calendar link for this story is 2nd April which is International Children's Book Day.

Hymn suggestion

Come and Praise Vol 1 'The Family of Man' No 69

Prayer

Let us bow our heads and think this morning about how foolish it is to waste time and effort being envious of what other people have.

Let us pray that we can be contented people; let us give thanks for the good things in our lives; let us remember all those who are less fortunate than we are. Amen.

National Curriculum cross-curricular reference

A quite far-reaching project in Geography and/or Science which could be initiated by this story would be to choose from very different areas of the world – a Pacific island as in the story, a desert region, a polar area, a congested inner-city area – and consider the different kinds of difficulties people living in these locations face.

There are plenty of possibilities for drama in this story and it is a good one for devising, or selecting, appropriate background music.

55 *This month*

Introduction

Many people think April is the most exciting month of all. To be outside is to see signs of spring all over, on land, on water and in the air. Perhaps one of the best ways to describe April is to say that it is the month of promise.

This month

April is the month when we think particularly about two birds. The first is the swallow and these birds can be seen arriving in April. Long ago when people didn't know so much about hibernation they thought swallows spent the winter months hiding in mud at the bottom of ponds!

Here is a poem about swallows:

> The swallow, for a moment seen,

Skim'd this morn the village green;
Again at eve, when thrushes sing,
I saw her glide on rapid wing
O'er yonder pond's smooth surface, when
I welcom'd her back again.
(Anon.)

The cuckoo also comes in April and his song is heard most often during this month and May. Many people think that cuckoos are scarcer these days but in fact it is just that they find it harder to get a home. Where hedges have been cleared, perhaps for building, the nests of birds like hedge sparrows and meadow pipits have been swept away with the hedge. Where once the uninvited cuckoo used to use nests like these for rearing, now he has to look further afield.

There are many old traditions associated with cuckoos. For instance, you should take careful note of what you are doing when you first hear the cuckoo call. An old tale says that what you are doing then will be what you will do for the rest of the year!

April is associated with showers and one of the worst ever floods occurred on 17th April 1421 when nearly a hundred Dutch villages were flooded and one hundred thousand people were drowned, lost or injured. On a more cheerful note, we can remember another saying: 'April showers bring May flowers.'

April, of course, has its own flowers too. Cow parsley, primroses, cowslips and dog violets start to appear and attract bees and wasps. Trees start to 'burst out' at this time of year and a close look at them will often show squirrels busily racing about building their nests, known as 'dreys'.

Near their sets young badgers come out to play at dusk and newts are safely wrapping their eggs in the leaves of water plants.

Probably no month has had as many poems written about it as April. Here are just two, which cheerfully tell that spring is here:

For lo, the winter is past,
The rain is over and gone;
The flowers appear on the earth;
The time of the singing of birds is come.
(Song of Solomon 11, 11–12)

But a little while ago
All the ground was white with snow;
Trees and shrubs were dry and bare,
Not a sign of life was there;

Now the buds and leaves are seen
Now the fields are fresh and green,
Pretty birds are on the wing
With a merry song they sing!
There's new life in everything!
How I love the pleasant Spring!
(Anon.)

Information for the teacher

1 Both the swallow and the cuckoo had days designated to them in times past. Old calendars noted 15th April as Swallow Day in Britain – presumably because this date was significant for increased sightings of the returning bird.

   20th April was the cuckoo's day and there are several other 'traditions' associated with hearing this bird's first song, as well as the one mentioned in the text. For girls, the number of times they heard a cuckoo call was the number of years they would have to wait before marriage. On a gloomier note for older people, the number of bursts of song indicated the number of years they had left to live!

2 Grass snakes can be seen near water at this time of the year and April is the month when adders perform their dance of courtship.

Hymn suggestion

Come and Praise Vol 1 'Think of a world without any flowers' No 17

Prayer

Dear God,
Thank you for another month which gives us so much to see and listen to and learn about. Help us to use our senses so that we can enjoy the natural things around us. Amen.

National Curriculum cross-curricular reference

Science would be well served by further investigation and observation of the features mentioned in the text.

   There is also plenty of opportunity for varied musical appreciation this month too. This might range from 'April Showers' and 'April in Paris' to *On hearing the first cuckoo in Spring* (Delius) and *Rite of Spring* (Stravinsky).

With so much poetry in the text this might be an opportunity to get the children to write some, possibly after some outdoor experience of the things talked about.

56   Mother Samwell

Introduction

One of the things that annoys all of us is being accused of doing something wrong which we haven't done. 'It's not fair,' we say straight away. Unfortunately, for many people hundreds of years ago, life was far from fair – as we can hear in this morning's story of Mother Samwell.

Story

The courtroom was crowded and the jury listened carefully as one witness after another told his or her story.

'Well, it was like this . . .' started a tall, burly man with a round red face.

'Yes – go on,' said the judge.

'Well, I was out riding one day and that . . . that . . . person was walking along a path in front of me.'

As he said this the burly man nodded his head in the direction of a frail, rather bent and tired-looking old woman who stood in the dock reserved for prisoners on trial. The woman was known as Mother Samwell.

'She was slow to get out of the way as we galloped towards her – so I shouted to her.'

'What did you say?'

'Well . . . I said . . . I mean . . . I said, "Get out of the way, you old witch." '

'And what happened?'

'Nothing, at the time, and after our usual hard ride I stabled my horse. Next morning when I went for him – there he was lying dead on the ground. Now – it's obvious, isn't it? She put a curse on him, she did. She's a witch all right – and this proves it.'

So the trial went on. More and more stories like this one were told. Parents told of their children being ill after calling rude names at Mother Samwell. Then there was the case of the old lady's badly burned arm. When she had first been accused of being a witch a group of local people had set about proving her innocence. 'It's quite straightforward,' said one of them. 'All you do is put one of her arms in boiling water. If it heals up in a week she's innocent, if not . . .'

When Mother Samwell's arm had been plunged into the boiling water she had fainted with the pain of it – and the arm was still swollen and blistered.

'Agnes Samwell, you have been found guilty of witchcraft. You, your husband and daughter will all be hanged.'

With a pitifully weak cry old Mother Samwell sank to the floor. Through her tears she protested her complete innocence. It was no use – she, her husband and daughter were duly hanged.

Information for the teacher

1 The trial of Agnes Samwell took place in Huntingdon on 4th April 1593. The last 'witch' to be executed in Britain was Janet Horne in 1727.
2 'It's not fair' and the evils of superstition can both lead on to a comparison of life 'then and now'. Such a comparison shows the unreasoning cruelty of times past in situations like this.
3 There are several other examples of unreasonable behaviour and unfair situations from the past. Early aboriginal women in Australia settled arguments by hitting each other with sticks. They took it in turn to land a blow and the one who survived longest was 'right'. In Nigeria an accused thief was only considered innocent if a duck's feather could be stuck through his tongue and come out without sticking.

A similar test to the 'arm in boiling water/healing in seven days' test of this story was making the accused walk on red-hot ploughshares. Again innocence was 'proved' if the feet were completely healed in seven days.

Hymn suggestion

Come and Praise Vol 1 'From the darkness came light' No 29

Prayer

Let us give thanks this morning that in Britain today people are no longer punished because of fearful superstitions. Let us give thanks for our schools where we can learn that there are no such things as witches and evil spells. Amen.

National Curriculum cross-curricular reference

History could be very well served by this subject. Much interesting research could be done on witches, and the development of crimes and punishments through the ages.

An 'it's not fair' theme is always one which appeals to primary-age children. It makes for excellent discussion material and can generate interesting written work, often of a first-hand nature. There are also opportunities for drama here.

57   Ruswarp the faithful

Introduction

Sometimes humans can learn a lot from the behaviour of animals – as this morning's story shows.

Story

The early April weather was ideal for walking. The air was fresh and the sun shone brightly out of a clear blue sky.

'This is the place to be when the weather is like this,' said the walker to himself as he climbed slowly up the mountain path of a lonely but beautiful part of Wales. 'Nobody about, peace, fresh air and . . .'

The walker's thoughts were interrupted by a sudden faint whine.

'Why, that sounds like a dog,' he thought. 'But how would a dog get out here?'

With the stones and pebbles of the path slipping beneath his boots, the walked climbed higher – and nearer to the faint noises of the dog. Finally, on turning a bend in the path, he was shocked to see the creature which was making the noise.

There, lying just alongside the path, was a brown and white collie. Piteous whimpers came from the dog's mouth and he was obviously too weak to stand. His body was so thin that his bones were almost sticking through the skin and his nose had the dryness of a very weak or sick dog.

'But what are you doing here, old chap?' asked the walker, getting down to stroke the poor dog's head. 'It's a bit of a mystery, isn't it?'

Sometime later the mystery was solved.

Not far from the starving dog the dead body of a man was found. Experts later decided that the man had been dead for three months, and this solved more of the mystery.

In January a man called Graham Nuttall, who was a keen hill walker, travelled from his house in Lancashire to walk in Wales. He told a friend that he would be back later that day and when he didn't arrive the police and rescue teams were alerted. Despite a search of the area, neither the man nor his dog, Ruswarp, could be found.

What had happened was that the man had fallen, become unconscious and finally died. Ruswarp, his fourteen-year-old collie, decided that the best thing to do was wait by his master until help arrived. He waited, guarding Mr Nuttall's body, for three months, drinking water from a nearby stream, but – as far as anybody could tell – going without food.

Despite his sadness at losing his master, the faithful Ruswarp's story had a happy ending. He was so weak that he had to be carried down the mountainside, but once safe he began to make a good recovery.

'We don't quite know how this wonderfully loyal dog managed to stay alive,' said a member of the RSPCA. 'We would expect a dog of his age to be able to stay alive in the wild for about five or six weeks with water and without food. But for three months . . .! He's a remarkable dog, this Ruswarp!'

Information for the teacher

1 Mr Nuttall came from Burnley and had taken the train to Llandrindod Wells on 20th January. His body was found in a stream near to where the dog was lying.
2 This story could provoke thoughts on the treatment of animals by humans. A useful quotation here might be: 'God places animals in our care – to reject them or treat them cruelly is to do wrong in the eyes of God.' (Muhammad)
3 A possibly useful address here is: RSPCA, The Causeway, Horsham, West Sussex RH12 1HG.
4 Readers may notice a great similarity to the famous story of the Scottish dog, Greyfriars Bobby. He displayed similar loyalty to his master in Scotland in the nineteenth century. His story is told in *Greyfriars Bobby* by Lavinia Derwent (Puffin).
   There is also a useful selection of stories about the devotions of

dogs in the *Guinness Book of Pet Records*, ed. Gerald L Wood (Guinness).

Hymn suggestion

Come and Praise Vol 1 'All the creatures of our God and King' No 7

Prayer

Dear God,
Thank you for all the love, faithfulness and loyalty of our pets. Give us the grace to treat them as they deserve. Amen.

National Curriculum cross-curricular reference

Science could certainly be involved in a further examination of the care of pets, their basic needs, the durability of dogs, etc. There is considerable scope for creative writing in English if looking at this story from Ruswarp's viewpoint. The location of the various places involved could be a useful geographical exercise and a 'History of Loyalty' file might be completed to give a historical survey of dogs through the ages.

58   *Don't leave it too late*

Introduction

There are lots of times when we look back and say, 'I *wish* I'd done that.' This morning's story makes us think even more about this.

Story

It was April weather at its wettest. There was a freezing cold wind blowing, and heavy rain blanketed the whole market place in an atmosphere of gloom. The stall holders huddled under cover and looked round for the few customers who were about.

'What a day!'

'We'll be lucky to sell anything today.'

'Nobody's going to turn out in this.'

'Have you seen him – over there?'

The stall holders looked over to a place in the market where old Bill Johnson's stall had stood for years. He had been dead for a long time now and no one had ever put up a new stall there. Today, however, a man was standing on the very spot where the stall had stood for so long. He wasn't looking round, or trying to shelter from the downpour. He wore no hat and his clothes were black with rain. His unmoving feet were set firmly in a large puddle.

'Who is he?'

'I've never seen him before.'

'He's not a customer . . .'

'. . . and he's certainly not a stall holder.'

'Just a minute, just a minute – it's old Bill Johnson's son, I'm sure of it.'

'What's he doing down here? He never came near the place when his father was alive. What's he doing here now?'

'There's only one way to find out. Let's ask him.'

The curious stall holders left their shelter and gathered round the drenched figure.

'Samuel – isn't it?' said one of them.

'Yes,' replied Samuel Johnson. 'I know you'll be wondering what I'm doing here, so I'll tell you.

'Years ago my father was sick and he couldn't look after his stall for a few days. He asked me to help. I wasn't working at the time and I could easily have done it. But I was far too proud to look after a market stall – I thought it was beneath me.

'Now my father is dead and I can't tell him how sorry I am that I let him down. The next best thing seemed to be to come down here and stand in the rain – perhaps somehow he'll know I'm trying to say sorry.'

The stall holders looked at each other without speaking. Then one of them said, 'You're very welcome to come and shelter with us.'

Information for the teacher

1 Dr Samuel Johnson (1709–84) was born in Lichfield, the son of a poor market bookseller. Johnson was acutely conscious of his poverty when he went up to Oxford. On one occasion a benefactor

left a pair of new shoes at his door after having seen the appalling state of the shoes Johnson was wearing. The new pair was angrily returned. He moved to London 'with twopence halfpenny in my pocket'.

In later life Dr Johnson was renowned for his kindness to the poor and the destitute.

He owes his immortality to James Boswell's *Life of Johnson*, published in 1791.

2 The theme of this story is always contemporary and could lead on to discussion among the children about their own experiences.

3 A Bible story with sufficient points of similarity and comparison is, of course, the Prodigal Son (Luke 15, 11–32).

Hymn suggestion

Come and Praise Vol 2 'When your Father' No 73

Prayer

Let us pray this morning about the mistakes we make in the way we behave.

Let us try always to see the other person's point of view as well as our own.

Let us remember that every job is worth doing well and that even though it is sometimes hard, we should be prepared to help wherever and whoever we can. Amen.

National Curriculum cross-curricular reference

There is obviously a great deal of historical scope in looking more thoroughly into the life and times of Samuel Johnson.

The RE aspect could be investigated further by a consideration of 'appearance', for Johnson was an extremely unattractive man physically (he suffered from scrofula and was very overweight) who had many inner qualities.

Many of his sayings could provoke discussions in English, although they may have to be adapted for use with young children. ('When a man is tired of London he is tired of life'; 'In human life much has to be endured, a little enjoyed.')

59 Learning a lesson

Introduction

At some time or other we have all done something we wish we hadn't. This morning's story is quite a funny one but it helps to remind us that a guilty conscience is not something we want.

Story

'This way we'll get rid of him forever,' said Brer Rabbit.

'Well . . .' muttered Brer Bear.

'Of course, don't you see?' went on Brer Rabbit. 'We set fire to his house, nobody will know we've done it, and we'll be rid of him forever.'

So the plotters decided to get rid of their arch enemy, Brer Anansi.

That night they crept through the woods to his house. Making sure nobody was about, they piled dry branches round the trunk of the tree and set the whole thing on fire. The flames shot skywards, smoke billowed through the wood and within a very short time the tree in which Anansi had his home was just a blackened stump.

'That's the end of him,' smirked Brer Rabbit. 'Let's go and celebrate.'

Next morning the plotters met together to have a feast. At last they had got rid of that pest Anansi. Soon the pots were boiling and Brer Rabbit bent over them smelling the delicious food. Brer Bear dozed nearby. Then a third figure appeared in the clearing – Anansi.

He had of course not been in his house when it burnt down. On returning from spending the night with a friend, he had found the wreckage of his home and assumed that it had been destroyed by lightning. Now he was collecting a large piece of wood to build a new house. He had been on his way to do this when the lovely smell had tempted him to the clearing.

He was just about to speak when Brer Rabbit turned from his pots. Seeing Anansi he gave a terrified gasp, dropped everything and fled into the forest.

'Strange,' thought Anansi. 'What peculiar behaviour.'

At that moment Brer Bear saw Anansi coming towards him with a large piece of wood.

'Aaaaah,' cried Brer Bear, 'he's come back to take his revenge!'

With that, he leaped onto a donkey and fled. A piece of wood at the end of the donkey's tether kept hitting Brer Bear and he was sure that the ghost of Anansi was in pursuit, beating him with the stick.

So the two plotters fled and did not return for weeks. Meanwhile Anansi thoroughly enjoyed their feast.

Information for the teacher

1 Stories of Anansi the trickster abound. Originally a West African legendary figure and supposed creator of the world, he has achieved a more international status while remaining a cultural hero. Only with the Wax Girl does he meet his match.
2 The early reference to fires in this story could direct things to a different and more serious tack if the teacher wishes. The danger of fires might be linked with fire brigades in a 'people who help us' theme. A useful address in this context might be: Chief Officer (Public Relations), London Fire Brigade Headquarters, 8 Albert Embankment, London SE1 7SD.
3 A possible calendar link here is that on 13th April 1695, Jean de la Fontaine, one of the most famous of all fable writers, died in France. In similar vein Hans Andersen was born on 2nd April 1805.

Hymn suggestion

Come and Praise Vol 1 'God knows me' No 15

Prayer

Dear God,
We pray that you may give us the wisdom to think before we act. In this way, may we be free from doing something about which we will be very sorry later. Amen.

National Curriculum cross-curricular reference

The 'guilty conscience' theme is one which usually stimulates a good response in discussion with children of primary school age. They might be encouraged to write 'anonymous' examples of something they have done, following such a discussion. This again is a good story to dramatise.

A more serious consideration of fire, combustible materials, prevention of fires and action to extinguish them could be pursued in both Science and Technology and there is obvious scope for controlled practical work here.

60 Don't count your chickens before they're hatched

Introduction

The title of this morning's story is a warning, as you will find out when you listen to the story of Hannah.

Story

Hannah lived many years ago in the country. She milked cows, raised chickens and hens – and dreamed.

'Ah, if only . . . Wait until . . . That'll be the day.'

Such thoughts were often going through her head when she went about her jobs. One of these jobs was taking a can of milk to the local market to sell. She always carried the can balanced on her head. This particular day the can was very big and very full.

'Aha,' thought Hannah, as she walked along. 'I'll get quite a bit of money for this milk. When I've got it I'll go straight away and buy some more eggs.'

Pausing in her thoughts, she carefully climbed over a fence, holding the milk can carefully on her head. Once she was on the other side, she set off quickly, avoiding the big stones on the path. Her mind slipped off into its daydreams once again.

'Yes. I'll get some eggs and then, along with the ones I've already got, they should give me about two or three hundred chickens. I'll wait until the market prices are at their highest for chickens and then I'll bring them all to market. Now, let's see – two hundred and fifty chickens at a good price will give me . . .'

At that moment a farmer's dog came bounding up to Hannah, barking excitedly. She held on to the milk can firmly with one hand, and shooed the dog away. Seeing that she wasn't interested in playing, the dog soon trotted off, leaving Hannah to get on her way – and continue her thinking.

'Now, where was I? Oh yes, I've just sold two hundred and fifty chickens at the market for a good price. It will be more than enough for me to buy a lovely new dress.'

By now Hannah had fallen in step with quite a few other people who were walking to the market. She smiled at them but made no attempt to talk – she was far too busy with her thoughts!

'That lovely new dress. Right. It'll be blue to match my eyes. It'll have a long, full skirt and puffy sleeves and by the time I get it the great fair won't be too long off. I'll wear it to the fair and when there's dancing all the young men will come and ask me for a dance. But I'll be waiting for someone special so I'll just shake my head . . .'

So wrapped up in her thoughts was Hannah that she *did* shake her head – and the milk can crashed to the ground, emptying its contents all over the stony path.

Information for the teacher

1 This story is adapted from one of Aesop's fables. A useful story from the Bible to parallel this is the tale of the man who built bigger and better barns, filled them with produce so that he could retire and enjoy the 'good life' and died the night of his retirement. (Luke 12, 16–20)

A useful Biblical reference in connection with both stories might be:

> Be most careful how you conduct yourselves:
> Like sensible men, not like simpletons.
> (Ephesians 5, 15)

2 A most dramatic, and tragic, real-life story of 'counting chickens' concerned the sinking of the *Titanic*. This took place in the early hours of 15th April 1912.

Hymn suggestion

Come and Praise Vol 1 'The wise may bring their learning' No 64

Prayer

Let us think this morning about taking care of the small things in our lives. Let our dreams not get in the way of what we should be doing now.

Let us pray that we might be reliable, sensible people who never let our friends and relatives down.

To help remind us about these things let us listen to the words of a poem:

For want of a nail a shoe was lost
For want of a shoe a horse was lost
For want of a horse a rider was lost
For want of a rider a battle was lost
For want of a battle a kingdom was lost
And all for the want of a horseshoe nail.

(This poem is by Benjamin Franklin and relates to the death of Richard III.)

National Curriculum cross-curricular reference

A little research beforehand by the teacher could result in a collection of well-known 'sayings' being made. These could be compared with the title here and all would promote useful discussion material with the children. This could lead on to some creative writing of stories which illustrate a saying in much the same way as this adaptation of Aesop.

The progress of the girl carrying the milk in this story is an interesting vehicle for some improvised music to reflect her progress, interruptions, dreams and ultimate disaster.

The question of balance and balancing could be used to stimulate work in Science and the financial aspect of the 'dream' could provide for some lighthearted but interesting work in Maths.

Section B
Class assemblies

This section contains a group of fully-prepared *celebratory class assemblies*. There are suggestions linking them to significant times in the term.

Each assembly is detailed in terms of aims, materials required, calendar location, numbers involved, preparation, information and presentation.

Where there are playscripts for direct use with the children these are provided in bigger print and can be used for photocopying.

One of the general aims of this section is to produce a detailed resource which requires the minimum of preparation but provides for dramatic and thought-provoking assemblies.

1 The best time is now

Aim: to focus the children's attention on an admirable quality – in this case, honesty.

Materials required: depend on how the dramatic part of the assembly is presented. The character parts could be read by one group of children while others mime the action; alternatively, a group could read the play with pictures or overhead projections illustrating the action.

Numbers involved: whole class participation

Calendar location: January

Information and preparation: Class assemblies need adequate preparation and to locate one in January means that it should be effective without making too many demands in the way of complex presentation. This assembly requires very little preparation but it has proved very effective.

The play is based on a true story and the children were not only rewarded materially, but were commended for their honesty too.

The concluding prayer of the assembly is a very much adapted piece from the Sanskrit.

Presentation

The audience could enter the hall to some music which evokes optimism, a light touch and cheerfulness. (Perhaps Mozart's *Eine kleine Nachtmusik*.) Once the audience is in position some speakers from the presenting group could effect the introductions:

SPEAKER 1: January gets its name from the Roman god, Janus. Janus was the god of doorways and beginnings. He had two heads – one to look backwards at the time past, and the other to look forward to the future.

SPEAKER 2: January is supposed to be a time when mistakes and bad things are left behind and we make new starts when this is necessary.

SPEAKER 3: January is a time to think about all those qualities which we admire – kindness . . .

SPEAKER 2: . . . friendship . . .

SPEAKER 1: . . . reliability . . .

SPEAKER 2: . . . honesty . . .

SPEAKER 1: Yes, honesty – and now we're going to introduce you to some people.

SPEAKER 3: Here they are. (*The characters come on as announced*.) There's Lee, Elliott, Emerson, Donna, Fay, Emma, Nicola and Police Sergeant Lester.

SPEAKER 2: Sometimes all these children visited a rubbish dump. It was piled high with all sorts of things – old bikes, chairs, broken TV sets, and wardrobes. Now listen to what happened there . . .

LEE: We shouldn't be here.

EMERSON: Why not?

ELLIOTT: Because my mum says it's dangerous to play on rubbish dumps.

DONNA: Mine does, too.

EMERSON: Yeah – you've got to be careful. But I know a boy who found a bike. All it wanted was two new tyres and it was as good as new.

FAY: Think we'll find any bikes today?

EMMA: We might find something good.

NICOLA: Not if we talk all day – let's get looking.

LEE: Look, here's an old suitcase.

ELLIOTT: Anything good inside?

LEE: No, just a load of old clothes.

EMERSON: Anybody want a washing machine, or a telly with no screen in?

FAY: Just a load of old rubbish here.

EMMA: Well, what do you expect? It is a rubbish dump, after all.

EMMA: Hang on, I'm going to have a look at that pile of furniture over there.

LEE: What for – want a new bed?

(ALL *laugh*.)

EMERSON: I can see a wardrobe. I'm going to have a look in it.

ELLIOTT: Looks to me as if it's been there for fifty years.

DONNA: Be careful, Emerson, that pile doesn't look safe.

FAY: I can just see the headlines – 'Boy finds space suit in dumped wardrobe'.

EMERSON: You lot won't laugh if I find something.

EMMA: Go on then, get the door open and look inside.

EMERSON: It's not as easy as you think. This door hasn't been opened for ages – *uhh* – come on, open up!

NICOLA: It's coming, Emerson – it's opening.

EMERSON: You're right. (*Loud creaking noise.*)

ELLIOTT: Watch out for ghosts.

EMERSON: Never mind ghosts, there's something on the top shelf in here . . .

LEE: What is it?

EMERSON: Oh, it's just a pile of papers . . . hang on . . .

DONNA: Hang on . . . what?

EMERSON: There's an old envelope wedged in between some of the papers. It isn't half fat.

FAY: Bring it down here.

EMMA: Then when you open it we can all see.

NICOLA: This is a bit scary.

ELLIOTT: No it's not, it's exciting. Ah, here it is.

EMERSON: OK – now let's have a look.

LEE: There's more paper inside.

NICOLA: It's wrapped round something.

EMERSON: Cor . . . it's . . . it's . . . money!

FAY: How much?

EMERSON: Tons and tons of it – look!

ELLIOTT: Let's count it – it's all in £20 notes.

EMERSON: Right – Lee, Donna, Fay, Emma, you count this pile. Elliott and Nicola, help me count my pile.

LEE: £20 . . . £40 . . . £60 . . . £80 . . .

EMERSON: £20 . . . £40 . . . £60 . . . £80 . . .

(*A minute or two later . . .*)

LEE: We've finished.

ELLIOTT: How much have you got?

DONNA: Three thousand, two hundred pounds.

FAY: How much has your group got?

NICOLA: We've got two thousand and eight hundred pounds.

EMERSON: That's . . . six thousand pounds we've got!

ELLIOTT: We can buy . . . *dozens* of bikes!

DONNA: Or videos . . . or CDs . . . or . . . or *anything*!

EMMA: We're rich, we're rich!

EMERSON: Hang on, hang on, it's not ours. The money doesn't belong to us.

ELLIOTT: But we found it, didn't we?

DONNA: It would probably have been burned but for us.

LEE: Yeah, and . . .

EMERSON: No, whatever we say, it's not our money. We'll have to take it to the police station in Orchard Road.

SPEAKER 1: So the children went to the police station.

EMERSON: Excuse me, sergeant.

POLICE SERGEANT: Yes? Now what have you lot been up to?

LEE: We've found some money.

ELLIOTT: Yeah – lots and lots.

POLICE SERGEANT: Where did you find this?

DONNA: On the rubbish dump near Elm Street.

POLICE SERGEANT: You shouldn't be playing there, you know. It's dangerous. However, let's see the money.

EMERSON: Here it is, sergeant.

POLICE SERGEANT: Right . . . Dear oh dear! There's a fortune here.

FAY: We know, we've counted it. Six thousand pounds.

POLICE SERGEANT: OK. This is what happens. First of all I have to take down all the details – your names and addresses, how much was found and where you found it. Then we try and trace the owner. But whatever happens we'll be in touch with you again.

EMMA: Right-oh, sergeant.

ALL CHILDREN: Bye, sergeant!

POLICE SERGEANT: Not so fast, not so fast. Come back here, all of you.

EMERSON: What for, sergeant?

POLICE SERGEANT: Because I want to say how impressed I am at your honesty. You did the right thing by bringing the money back here – and somebody, somewhere, might be very grateful.

SPEAKER 2: A long time passed, during which the children heard nothing. Then, one day, they were asked to go to the local police station with their parents. When they got there they were told that nobody had claimed the money, and as a result they were to get £857.14p each! Not only had their honesty been rewarded but their story was told in all the newspapers.

SPEAKER 3: We are now going to sing the hymn: 'Make us worthy, Lord'. (*Come and Praise* Vol 2 No 94)

SPEAKER 1: Let us end our assembly this morning by thinking again about time. The time to do good deeds, to act well, to put mistakes right is not tomorrow or the next day or next week, it is now.

Listen to the following prayer which reminds us of this:

SPEAKER 2:

Look to this day
for it is the very way of life,
in its brief course lie all the real things of our lives;
the way we act,
how we grow,
good deeds and beautiful sights and sounds.
Yesterday is a dream, and tomorrow is a thought,
but today, well lived, makes every yesterday a dream of
    happiness
and every tomorrow full of hope.
Look well, therefore, to this day.

The service could then end with the same piece of music which served to introduce it.

2 *Fun for all*

Aim: by comment, spectacle, story and information to give the children a greater knowledge and appreciation of the Hindu spring festival of Holi

Materials required: some pre-assembly paintings; a few jars containing coloured powder paint; some jars containing coloured water; a bicycle pump; an outline map of India; some recorded Indian music

Numbers involved: whole class participation

Calendar location: late February/March

Information and preparation: Three of the main facets of the festival of Holi are colour, noise and spectacle. All three are immensely popular with primary-age children (!) but careful thought needs to be given as to how these can be reflected in assembly.

One suggested approach is for the teacher to read through the Presentation which follows and then prepare to adapt it according to choice, the age and ability of the presenting children, the constraints of the hall and the availability of materials.

Presentation

Once the audience has been assembled in the hall, the class giving the presentation could enter to the accompaniment of some Indian music being played on tape or record.

Two of the presenters could immediately step to the front and engage in the following repartee:

A: Today our assembly is about 3Rs.

B: Oh *no!* (*Groans*)

A: What do you mean – 'Oh *no*'?

B: Well, you do mean Reading, 'Riting and 'Rithmetic, don't you?

A: Of course I don't. I mean RANG, RAS and RAG.

B: What on earth is that?

A: Well it means COLOUR, DANCE and SONG. It's to do with the Hindu festival of Holi.

B: Hmmm . . . can you tell us more about that?

A: Certainly. Sit back, look and listen.
(*These two move back to allow five more children to step forward.*)
    (*Each of these five children holds a prepared piece of card on which are written words in large block capitals. These words are shown to the audience. They are: WHAT? WHEN? HOW? WHO? WHY? The children holding the cards each then offers a relevant comment about their card:*)
WHAT?: This morning we are going to tell you what the festival of Holi is.
WHEN?: We will tell you when it takes place.
HOW?: We will show you, in different ways, how people celebrate Holi.
WHO?: We will tell you who celebrates this occasion and also the people associated with Holi.
WHY?: Once you have seen our assembly we are going to leave you with some questions which you might talk about later in your own rooms.
WHAT?: Here are some facts about Holi: Holi is a Hindu festival which is sometimes called 'The Festival of Colour'. It is held in spring and celebrates the end of winter and the time when the first harvest of the year will begin. There is always a carnival atmosphere at Holi celebrations.
WHEN?: Holi is celebrated during an Indian month which is called Phalguna. This is at the same time as March in the Christian calendar. Holi lasts for five days.
HOW?: Everybody has great fun at Holi. These are some of the things that happen.

At this stage you could combine words/pictures/action. Bottles of coloured powder and coloured water could be shown to the audience. The audience will enjoy being told that both these items (in reality, coloured dyes) are thrown over as many people as possible during the celebrations. With adequate preparation (caretaker approval, clothing, etc!), an action example involving two children could take place here. The bicycle pump could then be shown – with the comment that it is often used to fire the water.
    Pictures of Holi celebrations, painted in advance of the assembly, could be shown here too. These might highlight the bonfires which

are also an important feature. After this it could be back to the speakers . . .

HOW?: Another thing that happens is that people listen to old Indian stories from a book called the Panchatantra. Some children are going to act one of these stories now. It starts beside a pool of water which is drying up. Two geese and a tortoise are there . . .

GOOSE 1: It's drying up – we'll have to leave.

GOOSE 2: Yes – our lovely pool. How sad that we must go.

TORTOISE: Go? *Go?* You mean just because this pool is drying up you will go and leave me?

GOOSE 1: Well . . . er . . . but . . .

GOOSE 2: But you can't fly.

GOOSE 1: No, of course you can't. So how could you possibly come with us?

TORTOISE: I know exactly how.

GOOSE 2: You do?

TORTOISE: We find a thin stick. Each of you puts an end in your beak and I grip the middle with my mouth. Then we fly to a new pool.

GOOSE 1: Great idea! But remember, you can't open your mouth until we land.

TORTOISE: As if I would!

HOW?: So the stick was found and the three friends took to the air. On their way to the new pool they had to fly over a town . . .

TOWNSMAN: Look – look in the sky.

TOWNSWOMAN: Those geese must be very tired, carrying a tortoise like that. I wonder which one of them had the brilliant idea.

TORTOISE: It was *my* id . . . aaa . . . *aaaaahhhh*!

HOW?: That tortoise – he just had to open his mouth to tell folks how clever he was! Well, after listening to stories like this people often get up to have a dance . . . like this.

At this point a very simple improvisation of an Indian dance could be done by the children – a procession in which there is rhythmic clapping and chants of 'Holi-hai, Holi-hai, Holi-hai.'

Nine of the children could then each take a placard with one of the following words and explanations on.

Rang, Ras, Rag	*colour, dance and song*
Phalguna	*a month in the Indian calendar*
Holi-hai!	*words shouted in celebration*
Prahlad	*an Indian prince*
Hiranya-Kasipu	*his evil father*
Vishnu	*a Hindu god*
Sambat	*God of the Year*
Kama	*a mischievous spirit*
Holika	*Sambat's loyal sister*

WHO?: Well, you've heard about What, When and How; now I'm going to tell you about some of the important people to do with Holi. (*The children show their placards.*) All these people are in different stories about Holi. For instance, the Year God, Sambat (*points to Sambat*), had a sister called Holika (*points to Holika*). She loved him so much that when he died she insisted on being burnt on his grave. So, because she loved him so much, Sambat was given his life back. This story is one reason why people light bonfires to celebrate Holi.

(Much more could be made of this story if the teacher so wishes.)

At this point in the assembly the presenters could all come together again and, at a pre-arranged signal, say chorally: 'WHY?' A speaker might then advance with some questions for follow-up work, debate and discussion in the classrooms:

1 Why do we have festivals?
2 Do other religions have festivals at this time of year?
3 Are there other festivals like Holi?
4 Why is spring important?

The service could be ended by everybody singing hymn 72 from *Come and Praise* Vol 1.

As a final touch to end the service in a thought-provoking manner the presenting children could parade with the series of nine placards before, and as, the rest of the children leave the hall.

3 What was it like?

Aim: By means of comment, drama and illustration, to provide a picture of what life was like in Jerusalem at the time of the crucifixion

Materials required: appropriate 'Eastern' clothing for actors (very simple); chart for illustration of temple; background music as appropriate

Numbers involved: whole class participation

Calendar location: March/April

Information and preparation: This assembly requires little preparation and is a useful vehicle for setting the scene for further work in either the classroom or another assembly. The next class assembly in this book would be an ideal follow-up and together they could provide a satisfying and informative two-part look at Easter.

Presentation

The service could begin with everybody singing the hymn 'Trotting, trotting' (*Come and Praise* Vol 2 No 128). Following this a NARRATOR could introduce the service:

NARRATOR: In school we learn a lot about what happened in Jerusalem at the first Easter. We know that Jesus was betrayed by Judas Iscariot, that he was crucified on Good Friday and rose on Easter Sunday.

We don't know so much about what it was actually like in and around Jerusalem at this time, though. To put this right we have asked our school's interviewer to talk to some people who were there . . .

(*At this point some appropriate background music could be played. The* NARRATOR *leaves centre stage and is replaced by the* INTERVIEWER, *complete with microphone, and a 'young man',* ISAAC, *dressed in the simple cloak of Biblical times.*)

INTERVIEWER: Good morning, everybody. I'd like to introduce you to Isaac, who travelled to Jerusalem shortly before Jesus's arrival there.

ISAAC: Good morning.

INTERVIEWER: Now, Isaac. Please answer a few questions for

us. Why did crowds go to Jerusalem, and what was it like getting there?

ISAAC: Well, we Jews were expected to visit the temple in Jerusalem three times a year – for the feasts of the Passover in spring, Pentecost in summer, and the Tabernacles in the autumn.

It was great fun going to the city. Whole families travelled together and the roads were full of camels, donkeys, adults, children – all on their way to the city.

INTERVIEWER: What were the crowds like?

ISAAC: Great! Everybody was glad to be in one because if you travelled alone or in ones or twos you were much more likely to be attacked by robbers.

You saw old friends too, and there were constant shouts of greeting. And of course the singing! You should have heard that – you probably know some of the songs we used to sing – they are called psalms now.

INTERVIEWER: What were the roads like?

ISAAC: Dusty – dusty – and dusty! You got dust up your nose and in your hair. But they were in their best condition before the Passover festival because for a month before this workmen repaired all roads and bridges leading to the city.

We didn't have any photographs in those days – but my friends will show you what it was like . . .

(*At this point a group of Isaac's 'friends' appear at one side of the presenting area and move across the front of it. They are appropriately dressed, are shouting and singing (perhaps a simple phrase from a psalm) and several are playing simple flutes which were very common among Jews at this time. Isaac joins them.*)

INTERVIEWER (*speaking to the audience*): Now, we know that all these people were going to visit the temple in Jerusalem – but what was this temple like? Well, who better to tell us than Simon, who was a priest there.

(*Enter* SIMON, *the priest, who joins the Interviewer.*)

SIMON: Good morning, everybody. Well, the temple which Jesus knew was built about twenty years before he was born. It will be easier for me to tell you about it if you look at this plan.

(Simon then summons two helpers who unfurl a reproduction of the following plan of the temple.)

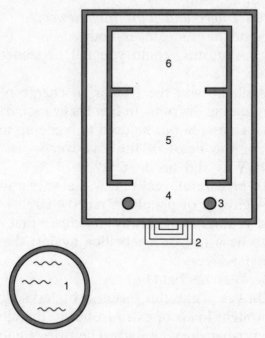

The Temple at Jerusalem

SIMON: Now, let me tell you as I point. Number 1 was a great bronze basin full of water. This is where we priests washed ourselves and all the holy objects we used.

Number 2 shows some steps leading up to the temple, which was about three metres higher than the courtyard round it. At the top of the steps were two great pillars – marked 3 – and the porch, which is marked 4.

Number 5 shows the Holy Place in the Temple – the golden seven-branched candlesticks were kept in here.

Then when you went into this area (*points to 6*), you were in the Holy of Holies. In a wooden box here was the Ark of the Covenant – that is to say, the writings of our Jewish Law.

INTERVIEWER: Thank you, Simon. (*Simon leaves*)

Now, one of the people we hear most about at Easter time is Pontius Pilate, but again we don't know very much about him or what his job was. This morning I am pleased to welcome

Augustus, a Roman soldier who worked closely with Pontius Pilate.

Good morning, Augustus.

(AUGUSTUS *enters and joins Interviewer*)

AUGUSTUS: Good morning, everybody.

INTERVIEWER: Augustus, could you tell us something about Pontius Pilate, please?

AUGUSTUS: Well, he was the Roman in charge of Jerusalem and the surrounding districts. In fact his headquarters were in a place called Caesarea but he used to come up to Jerusalem at the time of the Feast of the Passover.

INTERVIEWER: Why did he do that?

AUGUSTUS: To be careful, really. It was always a time of great excitement – crowds of people in narrow streets, everybody shouting and yelling. Pilate always reckoned that if there was ever going to be a riot or a rebellion against the Romans it would be at Passover.

INTERVIEWER: Was he right?

AUGUSTUS: Oh yes. Take this business of Jesus, for instance. Pilate had brought loads of extra troops to the city expecting trouble. Then what does he find? The priests and leaders of the Jews want him to execute one of their own people for them!

Pilate said to me afterwards, the only way to keep peace in the city was to sacrifice the Jewish preacher – although he couldn't see that he had done anything wrong at all.

INTERVIEWER: Thank you, Augustus. (*Augustus leaves*)

Today we get news from all over the world very quickly indeed – through television, newspapers, radio. But how did news get around in the time of Jesus? Please meet Mary.

Good morning, Mary. (*Enter* MARY)

MARY: Good morning, everybody.

INTERVIEWER: Could you tell us how news of those great events in Jerusalem was spread around?

MARY: Oh, yes. It had to be done by one person telling others what had happened. Jesus's disciples worked hard to tell as many people as possible about his great work. But things got very, very difficult.

INTERVIEWER: How do you mean?

MARY: Well, the early Christians had many enemies who wanted to stop them meeting and stop them talking – and often wanted to kill them.

Then, of course, the disciples were getting older.

INTERVIEWER: So what happened?

MARY: Well, Christian meetings became more and more secret – and then came a particularly important one. Now – look at these people . . .

(A group of people, 'men and women', come into the presentation area in groups of two or three. They gather together, mime talking animatedly – and a 'young man' is busy writing everything down.)

MARY: In the year 64 there was a terrible fire in Rome. Some people blamed Nero the Emperor for it and he wasn't having this! So he had to find somebody else to blame – naturally he chose the Christians!

As a result more and more Christians died and their secret meetings became very dangerous.

One of these Christians – the young man you see writing, who was called Mark – decided that he had better write down all he knew of the Jesus story. So, remembering much of what the disciple Peter had told him, he wrote an account of Jesus's life.

INTERVIEWER: Thank you, Mary. *(Mary exits along with mime group)* Now we know how the Gospel of St Mark came to be written and we know that three others – by Matthew, Luke and John – followed. *(Exit Interviewer)*

TEACHER: This morning we have learned more about the life and times of that first Easter.

Let us sing hymn number 129, 'Jesus in the Garden'. *(Come and Praise Vol 2)*

After the singing of this hymn the assembly could be ended with a prayer:

This morning we have been hearing what it was like at the time of the first Easter. Let us pray that the more we learn the more able we are to live in peace and happiness with each other. Amen.

4 Report from Jerusalem

Aim: to increase the children's awareness of the Easter story in a way which is interesting and appropriate to them

Materials required: the main format of this assembly is a commentary with illustrative support. The latter could be supplied in a number of ways:

a by means of an overhead projector with a series of consecutive transparencies. This has much to recommend it as the pictures can be clearly seen by the audience and are in an elevated position;

b if no overhead projector is available, a series of large pictures mounted on thick card could be used. The advantage here is that they could be added to as the service progresses and at the finale all will be in place – giving a composite picture of events;

c a third alternative is to use class members in costume tableaux arrangements to reflect each part of the story. An optional tape of background sounds could be used to add effects.

Numbers involved: whole class participation, certainly in preparation, and perhaps during the assembly

Calendar location: March/April

Information and preparation: The Easter story is always a difficult one for primary school children. As one of the two most important occasions in the Christian year it is still so complex that a majority of teachers feel uneasy in relating it to children of eleven and under.

One way of approaching this problem is to try to build up a background knowledge of the setting, with the dramatic events represented alongside this.

This may not bring the children any nearer to an understanding of Easter but it will portray to them how important this part of the Christian story is.

This assembly is prepared for use by itself but it might be even more effective if used as the second part of an extended look at Easter, with *Class Assembly 3* as its forerunner.

Presentation

The introductory music for the children entering the hall might be something modern – from *Jesus Christ Superstar* or

Godspell. When the audience is in place the first speaker could take up a prominent position in the presenting area and begin:

SPEAKER: This morning several of our reporters are going to tell you about what happened in Jerusalem at the time we now know as the first Easter. We will be looking at this chart from time to time. (*Points to the following chart, which appears on a large piece of card or overhead projector screen.*)

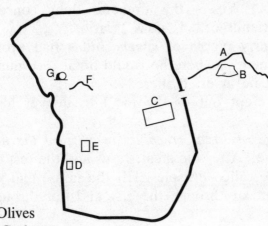

A Mount of Olives
B Garden of Gethsemane
C Temple
D Room where Jesus had Last Supper
E House of the High Priest
F Hill of Calvary
G Garden of the Tomb

Jerusalem at the time of Jesus

SPEAKER: Now, here is our first reporter.
REPORTER 1: My job was to cover the entry of Jesus into the city of Jerusalem – I can tell you it was like a carnival! Hundreds of people had heard of him and his great teaching and they turned out to give him a terrific welcome.

They cut branches off the trees and spread them in his path and when he came riding into the city on a donkey you could hear the cheers on the other side of the city.

(*Picture of Jesus's triumphal entry into the city. Background*

*music of cheering either from a tape or children 'off-stage'. If
doing tableaux, then a 'frozen group' of welcomers looking
into the distance.*)

REPORTER 2: Once in the city, Jesus and his friends went to
have a quiet meal together. The house they went to is
marked D on our chart so you can see it was here. (*Reporter
or teacher points to D*) At this house Jesus and his friends had
bread and wine – but a dreadful thing was already happening.

(*Picture of the Last Supper*)

REPORTER 3: Yes – this dreadful thing concerned one of
Jesus's friends called Judas Iscariot.

For thirty pieces of silver, Judas had promised to tell
Jesus's enemies where he would be at a certain time so that
he could be arrested there.

Judas crept out of the meal to deliver his treacherous
message.

(*Picture of Judas creeping away from the house*)

REPORTER 3: After the meal, Jesus and the rest of his friends,
who were called disciples, left the house and walked in the
cool night air through the city and out through one of its
gates.

They headed for a place called the Mount of Olives and
rested in a garden there. This garden was called Gethsemane
and you can see both the garden and the Mount of Olives on
our chart. (*Reporter or teacher points to A and B on chart*)

When they had been there for a while there was a sudden
commotion. Torches appeared in the distance and a group of
temple policemen and soldiers came noisily into the garden.

Judas was with them and he showed them which man was
Jesus. Jesus was roughly arrested and taken to the house of
the High Priest.

(*Picture of Jesus's arrest*)

REPORTER 4: You'll see that E marks the house of the High
Priest on our chart. Jesus was taken there and more dreadful
things happened.

The priests were jealous of his popularity, they thought he
was a troublemaker and they wanted him out of the way.
Even though he had done nothing wrong they wanted to take
him to the Roman governor for trial.

Peter, Jesus's closest friend, followed the soldiers to the High Priest's house to see if he could help. When he was challenged there he became frightened and said he didn't know Jesus. He was sorry about this for the rest of his life.

(*Picture or tableau showing Peter's denial*)

REPORTER 5: The next morning Jesus was taken before the Roman governor – a man called Pontius Pilate.

Pontius Pilate listened to what the priests said but he couldn't see that Jesus had committed any crimes. By now, however, the priests had got lots of people on their side and there were crowds shouting against Jesus.

'Hmmm,' thought Pilate. 'If I'm not careful here there will be a riot, and that would never do. I know it's wrong but perhaps the best thing would be to have this man executed – and then the people will settle down.'

So, after thinking all this, Pilate did two things. He agreed that Jesus could be executed, but he washed his hands in a bowl of water to show that he didn't really agree with what was happening.

(*Picture of Pilate washing his hands*)

REPORTER 6: Then Jesus was forced to carry a heavy cross through the streets, and was bullied. The soldiers treated him so cruelly and hurt him so much that he had to be helped to carry the cross. Jesus and his cross were taken to a place called the Hill of Calvary. (*Reporter or teacher points to F on the chart*)

(*Picture of a simple cross on a hill*)

REPORTER 7: On the Hill of Calvary, Jesus, and two men who were criminals, were nailed onto the crosses which were then put into holes in the ground to make them stand up.

Jesus died from his wounds on the cross. Then he was taken down and put in a sort of cave which was cut out of rocks in a nearby garden. (*Reporter or teacher points to G*)

REPORTER 8: Up to this point this has been a very sad story, but it suddenly changed. Two days later it was found that the rock which had covered the entrance to the cave had moved – and the cave was empty.

Jesus's friends were surprised, and worried, and then overjoyed. They believed he was alive again.

SPEAKER: Well, you've heard our reporters telling you about those dramatic happenings in Jerusalem so many years ago.

All over the world today, Christians celebrate the great festival of Easter.

TEACHER: Let us now sing an Easter hymn, thinking particularly about the words as we do so: hymn number 129. (*Come and Praise* Vol 2)

5   *Food for thought*

Aim: to learn more about a special time of year – Passover; to be aware of 'signs and symbols' in our lives

Materials required: a very simple model of some traffic lights; simple props for the 'Roman household'; cards displaying some significant words associated with the Passover feast

Numbers involved: whole class participation

Calendar location: April

Information and preparation: It would be a great help if a very simple model of traffic lights could be constructed to serve as appropriate visual material to be used in conjunction with the refrain: 'Red, Amber, Green.' Notation for this is as follows:

Red, Am—ber,   Green

The play used to depict the eve of Passover in a Jewish household will need pre-assembly preparation but the entire script for this is in the presentation section. The cards depicting some of the features of the Seder (Passover meal) could have illustrations as well as words on them if the teacher so wishes.

Presentation

The assembly could begin with only the model traffic lights, in position 'centre stage'. Once the audience has been settled, the presenting group could then enter singing, and clapping, to the 'Red, Amber, Green' melody.

Once everybody is in position this chant stops and a speaker makes the following comment:

SPEAKER: Traffic lights are symbols which pass a message on to us. Instead of singing 'Red, Amber, Green,' we could sing the following . . .

(*At this point, using the same melodic chant, and still clapping out the rhythm, the presenting class change the words to* 'DANGER, CAUTION, GO.' *This could be repeated several times before the speaker continues*.)

SPEAKER: Now, we know that red symbolises 'danger'; amber 'caution', and green 'go'. This morning's assembly is about a special time of the year for some people, when different kinds of symbols are very important to them. On the night before their special festival begins you might see the following taking place in a Jewish home.

(*At this point the presenting group could form a large semi-circle, within which a small group could perform a very short play depicting preparations in a Jewish family home just before Passover*.)

The night before Passover

Characters: NARRATOR, MR STEIN, MRS STEIN, REBECCA, LUKE and DAVID – who are twins.

NARRATOR: This morning we are going to look inside a Jewish home on a special night in the month of Nisan. The Jewish month of Nisan usually takes place around April. It is the night before the Passover festival begins and Mr and Mrs Stein are talking together . . .

(*Enter* MR STEIN *and* MRS STEIN)

MRS STEIN: Well, who has done the hiding this year?

MR STEIN: Rebecca – she's been busy for ages. I think we're going to have to look very hard! I still remember how much I enjoyed it as a child when it was my turn to hide the chametz.

MRS STEIN: I've just been reminding Luke and David what chametz is.

MR STEIN: What did you tell them?

MRS STEIN: I reminded them that our ancestors, when they fled from Egypt, didn't have time to let the bread rise. So we remember this time by getting rid of anything in the house which will make bread rise – such as yeast or self-raising flour – and we call all such things as that chametz.

MR STEIN: Such messy stuff – I always used to have a job hiding the trails it left when I hid it.

MRS STEIN: Not Rebecca!

MR STEIN: Where are they, anyway?

MRS STEIN: In their bedrooms. I told them we wouldn't start until it was completely dark.

MR STEIN: That's how it should be, of course. I suppose you've got the candle all ready for the search?

MRS STEIN: I certainly have, and the feather for sweeping up any chametz found and . . .

   (*Enter* REBECCA, LUKE *and* DAVID)

REBECCA: Mum, Dad . . . it's dark!

LUKE: It's pitch black!

DAVID: Can we start?

MRS STEIN: I think so . . . I'll go and get the candle and the feather.

   (*She goes off*)

MR STEIN: As soon as your mother gets back we'll have the blessing, and then, everybody start looking!

   (*Mrs Stein returns*)

MR STEIN: Blessed are you, Lord our God, King of the Universe, who brings forth fruit from the wine.

REBECCA: Right, you lot – get looking!

   (*The family starts to act out a rigorous search. As they are doing this, the* NARRATOR *speaks:*)

NARRATOR: And so began the first family game of the Passover. Here you can see the Stein family looking behind the TV, under the settee, on top of the bookshelf – anywhere that Rebecca might have hidden some chametz. When they have found it all they will save it until morning, when it is burnt. The house will then be completely free of chametz and the festival can really begin.

Once the short play is over, the assembly could progress to providing more information about the Passover feast. The link with symbols, introduced at the start, could obviously be maintained here.

SPEAKER 1: The Passover feast is a very special one for all Jews because it is the time when they remember how Moses led the people of Israel away from a life of slavery in Egypt.

SPEAKER 2: On the first evening of the eight-day Passover

festival, all the family gather for a very special meal. A spare place is often set for an unexpected guest.

SPEAKER 3: Several important and symbolic things are set out on the table.

(*At this point in the presentation a group of children could hold up cards naming – and perhaps illustrating – some of the items of the Passover Seder. These might include*:

MATZOH   (unleavened bread)
MAROR   (bitter herbs)
HAROSET   (sweet herbs)

SPEAKER 1: During the Passover feast the youngest child asks the father of the family four questions. These are answered by the father, using a book called the Haggadah.

SPEAKER 2: The questions and answers are these . . .

SPEAKER 3: The youngest child asks: 'Why do we eat Matzoh?'

SPEAKER 1: Father answers: 'To remind us that our ancestors were slaves in Egypt. They had no time to let the bread rise when they fled.'

SPEAKER 2: The second question is: 'Why do we eat bitter herbs?'

SPEAKER 3: The answer is: 'The Egyptians made the lives of our ancestors bitter.'

SPEAKER 1: Question 3 is: 'Why do we dip twice?'

SPEAKER 2: Answer 3 is: 'First to taste the bitterness of slavery, and secondly to taste the sweetness of freedom.'

SPEAKER 3: Question 4 is: 'Why do we recline at our ease?'

SPEAKER 1: Answer 4 is: 'As a reminder that, like our ancestors, we can overcome slavery and bondage.'

The teacher could then interject and say that the story of the first Passover can be read in the book of Exodus (Chapter 12) in the Bible. In addition, if the children involved are old enough, an adaptation of the relevant passage could be read at this point.

Still contributing to the progress of the assembly, the teacher could then say that certain prayers are important to Jewish people, and could say two of them:

The Shema

Hear, O Israel, the Lord our God, the Lord is One, and you shall love the Lord your God with all your heart and with all your soul and with all your might.

The Exodus
>Therefore let us rejoice
>At the wonder of our deliverance
>From bondage to freedom,
>From agony to joy,
>From mourning to festivity,
>From darkness to light,
>From slavery to redemption,
>Before God, let us sing a new song.

Following the saying of these prayers, the teacher could continue: 'Jewish people are also famous as storytellers. Many of their stories are both amusing and have a good moral. Listen to this story as Class (*name of class*) act it for you.'

(This is one of those stories where a pre-recording of it on tape would have many advantages – differing voices and sound effects being at least two. As the taped story is replayed in the assembly, various children could mime the action involved. The story is ideal for this kind of presentation because it is simple, easy to dramatise, and has a pungent, humorous moral which requires no heavy-handed explanation.

The version which follows has deliberately been kept very short and simple, but it can be developed according to specific children's age and ability . . .)

One day Mrs Rosen went out shopping, leaving her husband in with a few friends. Shortly after she had gone, there was a knock at the door. On answering it, Mr Rosen found a beggar standing at the door.

Having no money in his pocket, and not knowing if there was any in the house, Mr Rosen was nonplussed at the beggar's plea for some small offering. Then, he remembered the old vase which stood at the end of the mantelpiece. That must be worth something! He gave it to the beggar.

A few minutes later Mrs Rosen returned. On hearing the story she was furious. Didn't Rosen know that the vase was a very valuable one, very valuable indeed! When he heard this

Mr Rosen ran to the front door and chased after the beggar. He soon caught him up.

Expecting the vase to be taken back from him, the beggar stood there forlornly.

'I've come to tell you something,' said Mr Rosen, panting. 'That vase is worth a great deal of money – don't let anybody cheat you when you sell it.'

The assembly might then continue with an appropriate Jewish saying, and an equally appropriate hymn. The saying could be: 'The world is preserved by three things: truth, justice, peace.'

The hymn could be 'The journey of life' (*Come and Praise* Vol 1 No 45).

When the hymn is finished a display of cards, showing the following information, could be brought out by the presenting class. These could then be taken to appropriate points in the hall so that the children can peruse them as they leave the hall. (The cards could later be displayed.)

Pesach	*Jewish name for Passover*
Haggadah	*the book used at the Passover meal*
Torah	*Jewish law (first five books of Old Testament)*
Seder	*the Passover feast*
Kiddush	*blessing spoken over the wine*
Chametz	*ingredients to make bread rise*

Section C
Anniversaries, facts, fancies, anecdotes and religious notes

Many assemblies can be developed from the fertile ground suggested by the above title. This section aims to provide a selection of such starting material.

The spring months

Introduction

Much of the information here will serve as source material for locally-developed assemblies. Where a particular event can be linked to an assembly (or assemblies) already detailed in this book, then there is an appropriate reference to aid teacher planning.

A note about the various calendars which govern the festivals of different faiths is important. *The Gregorian calendar*, which is solar-based and used in most western countries, enables most festivals related to this to be fixed. An exception is Easter, which is a movable feast. *The Jewish calendar* is lunar-based and to adjust it to the solar year an extra (embolismic) month is added seven times in each nineteen-year period. *The Islamic calendar* is lunar-based without adjustment, which means that Muslim festivals advance by some eleven to twelve days each year. More than one calendar has been in use in India.

The impact for teachers of these calendar fluctuations is that an annual plan of great religious festivals can only be accurately made by reference to the relevant current calendars. Otherwise it is a question of moving source material about as appropriate.

Throughout the comments which follow there are notes suggesting possible links with the detailed assemblies in the book.

January

> 'Then came old January, wrapped well
> In many weeds to keep the cold away.'
> (*Edmund Spenser, 1552–99*)

The ancient Jewish year, which began on 25th March, held its legal position in Christian countries up until the eighteenth century. It was not until 1752 that 1st January became the legal, as well as the 'popular' start to the English new year.

1st   This is the time for 'New Year Resolutions'. Charles Lamb said: 'The man who does not propose to himself to be better this year than he was last, must be either very good or very bad indeed.' (*Link – Assembly 1 and Class Assembly 1*)

The BBC began broadcasting its first programmes in 1927.

Traffic policemen were introduced in Great Britain in 1931.

In 1954 flashing indicator lights became legal requirements on all motor vehicles in Great Britain. (*Possible assembly starter for a 'signs' theme*)

2nd   The Roman poet Ovid died on this day in the year 18. He is remembered for many thought-provoking 'sayings': 'To be loved, be lovable' and 'While fortune smiles you will have a host of friends, but they'll desert you when the storm descends.'

General 'Tom Thumb' (real name Charles Stratton), probably the most famous dwarf, died in 1883. He was 31 inches (84cm) tall.

In 1914, at Hendon, a woman pilot looped the loop for the first time. Her name was Trehawke Davies. (*Link – Assembly 51*)

In 1984 a report said that acid rain was contaminating Britain's lakes and rivers.

3rd   In 1847 the Californian town of Yerba Buena had its name changed – to San Francisco.

On this date in 1661 Samuel Pepys noted in his diary that he had been to the theatre and that it was 'the first time that I saw women come upon the stage'. Prior to this, boys and young men had taken women's parts.

4th   During the Middle Ages monks compiled a catalogue of flowers for each day of the year, linking each flower with a saint. Today's flower is the common hazel and it is linked to St Titus.

Jacob Grimm (of the Grimm brothers' fairy tales) was born in 1785.

Louis Braille was born in 1809. He was three years old when an accident caused him to lose his sight. According to *The Young Louis Braille* by C H Abrahall, it was feeling the indentations on dominoes which was one inspiration for his devising the system known as Braille. (*Link – Assemblies 30 and 41*)

This was the date in 1944, during the Second World War, when Hitler ordered the mobilisation of all children over ten. (*Link – Assembly 32*)

5th   St Simeon Stylites died in 459. He lived for 36 years on a pillar 60 feet from the ground, wearing an iron collar and animal skins. Twice a day he preached to people who came to hear him. He was greatly admired for his patience, humility and wisdom. He was 69 when he died. (*Link – Assembly 8*)

In 1927 in New York the first demonstration of Movietone took place. This was a synchronisation of moving pictures and sound.

6th   This is the feast of Epiphany, which marks the time when three Wise Men first saw Jesus. 'Epiphany' comes from the Greek word which means 'appearance'. The Twelve Days of Christmas end with the Feast of Epiphany. In mediaeval England all twelve days were celebrated, with great festivities on the last night before serious work on the land began the next day. It is traditionally unlucky to have decorations up after Twelfth Night.

In 1928 the Thames burst its banks. Fourteen people were drowned, there was serious flooding and valuable paintings were damaged in the Tate Gallery.

In 1931, during excavations in Iraq, a royal palace dating from 550 BC was discovered.

In 1941 the world-famous pilot Amy Johnson was missing, believed drowned, after her plane disappeared while flying over the Thames Estuary. (Her body was never found.)

7th   In some parts of Japan this is a festival date on which rice cooked with herbs is eaten to prevent both bad luck and bad health.

8th   St Nathalan's Day. His generosity to others gained him sainthood but he is probably best remembered for losing his temper, then chaining his ankles in repentance. Throwing the key to his chains into the sea, he later bought a fish in Rome and, on cutting it open to cook, found the key inside. (*Link – Assembly 8*)

Galileo, the astronomer, died in 1642.

Elvis Presley was born in 1935.

9th   Davy's safety lamp was first used down a coal mine in 1816.

In 1920 the Government announced plans to build 100,000 new houses during the year.

In 1955 four hundred Jamaicans arrived in London to look for work.

10th   The Penny Post was introduced by Sir Rowland Hill in 1840.

'Buffalo Bill' (William F Cody) died in 1917.

'Tintin', the famous cartoon character, first appeared in Belgium in 1929.

After a twelve-day ordeal in which he tried to save his ship (the *Flying Enterprise*), Captain Henrick Carlsen had to abandon it forty minutes before it sank. This was in 1952 and was an early 'disaster' covered by TV. (*Link – Assembly 47*)

11th   Tradition has it that if today is mild moles start their tunnelling operations and throw up the first mole hills.

In 1905 the price of liner tickets to cross the Atlantic went up. To get from London to New York now cost £6.

12th   Charles Perrault was born in 1628. He wrote 'Cinderella' and 'Sleeping Beauty'.

In 1807 a ship full of gunpowder exploded at its moorings in the Dutch city of Leyden. One hundred and fifty-one people were killed and 2,000 injured, and 200 buildings were levelled. The blast was heard 50 miles away and the anchor of the ship was later found in a field outside the town.

Britain's first supermarket was opened in Manor Park in 1948.

13th   St Veronica died in 1497. She was a poor peasant girl who lived such an exemplary life that she became prioress of a nunnery. How the name Veronica came into being is significant. When Christ was carrying his cross a girl wiped his face with a cloth. After she had done so the cloth miraculously bore an imprint of his features – a *Vera Iconica* ('true portrait'). The cloth still remains in St Peter's in Rome.

During the 'flu epidemic of 1922, 804 people died during the week ending on this day.

14th   This is the feast day of St Kentigern, a Scottish saint whose Day is celebrated in Glasgow and elsewhere in Scotland.

On this date in 1205 one of the coldest ever spells hit Europe. A hard frost gripped England until 22nd March. From then on, 14th January was thought of as the coldest day of the year – something borne out in 1734 when Siberia registered temperatures of $-120°F$ and birds fell frozen from the sky.

Albert Schweitzer was born in 1875.

Lewis Carroll (author of *Alice in Wonderland*) died in 1898.

15th   This is the day on which St Paul, the first hermit, died in 342.

This is Martin Luther King Day in the USA. The civil rights leader was born in Atlanta, Georgia, in 1929. He was assassinated in Memphis, Tennessee, in April 1968.

16th   Promises! An advertiser said that on this day in 1749, at London's Haymarket Theatre, he would play sounds from every musical instrument on a walking stick, and would then squeeze himself into a quart bottle. A huge crowd bought tickets and turned up – but the 'magician' didn't. There was a riot and the theatre was wrecked. (*Link – Assembly 3*)

17th   This is the feast day of St Anthony, the patron saint of domestic animals, who died in 356. (*Link – Assemblies 14 and 50*)

On this date in 1939 the Nazi Government in Germany banned Jews from being dentists or vets and they were not allowed to drive cars, or go to cinemas and theatres.

18th   Every year on this date the festival of St Peter's Chair is held in Rome. This is held in St Peter's Church, where the chair on which the saint is said to have meditated is enshrined. The ceremony commemorates the founding of the papacy.

This is the date on which the annual week of prayer for Christian Unity begins.

Rudyard Kipling died in 1936.

In 1923, because of inflation, there were 112,000 Deutschmarks to £1. (*Link – Assembly 4*)

19th   James Watt, the inventor (steam engine), was born in 1736.

In 1903 a new bicycle race was announced in Paris – the Tour de France.

20th   This is St Sebastian's Day. Born in Narbonne, he was an early Christian who was killed by the Romans and buried under the Appian Way. During his life he managed to persuade one Roman governor to release many Christian prisoners. He lived during the third century.

John Howard, the prison reformer, died in 1790.

In 1961 John F Kennedy became the USA's youngest president. In his inaugural speech he said: '. . . ask not what your country can do for you; ask what you can do for your country.'

21st   This is the feast day of St Agnes (died 304). She is the patroness of purity.

In 1930 the BBC made the first world broadcast.

In 1935 Snowdonia, the first British National Park, was established. (*Link – Assembly 28*)

In 1987 Terry Waite, the Archbishop of Canterbury's special envoy, was kidnapped in Beirut.

22nd   Sir Francis Bacon, the great philosopher, was born in 1561. Despite his great mental powers, he was guilty of taking bribes when he was a judge. Hence the poet Alexander Pope described him as: 'The wisest, greatest, meanest of mankind'.

In 1901 Queen Victoria died at Osborne House on the Isle of Wight. She had reigned for 63 years.

In 1959 on this date it was announced that TV was growing rapidly in popularity and that two thirds of the British population now had a set. (*Link – Assembly 52*)

23rd   St Eusebius died in 400. He ate only once every four days.
        'Bodyline' bowling by the English cricket team in Australia caused great controversy.
        The first jumbo jet landed at London's Heathrow Airport in 1970.

24th   This is the feast day of St Timothy, bishop and martyr who was killed in 97 AD while trying to quell rioters in his temple.
        The Boy Scouts were founded by Baden Powell in 1908. (*Link – Assembly 28*)
        Winston Churchill died in 1965. He was ninety.

25th   This is the feast of St Paul and celebrates his conversion to Christianity. (Bible reference: Acts 9, 1–31) Tradition maintains that weather for the year can be foretold by how it is on St Paul's Day:

> 'If St Paul's Day be fair and clear,
> It does betide a happy year.'

        Robert Burns, the Scottish poet, was born in 1759. At Burns Night celebrations the haggis is eaten. The recipe for a haggis is minced heart and liver of sheep, suet, oatmeal, and seasoning – sewn into the sheep's stomach and boiled for three hours. (*Link – Assembly 18*)
        On this date in 1915 Alexander Graham Bell established a new long-distance record for a telephone call – 4,750 miles from New York to San Francisco. (*Link – Assembly 30*)

26th   Australia Day – commemorating the landing of Captain Arthur Phillips in 1788. On the same day in 1865 the sending of convicts from England to Australia ceased. (*Link – Assembly 38*)

27th   St John Chrysostum's Day. Born in 347 AD in Antioch, John was a brilliant orator ('Chrysostum' means 'golden mouth') whose Christian message made him enemies who succeeded in getting him banished. He died, ill and exhausted, while travelling in 407. Thus he was not a martyr but his sainthood came from his devotion and sincerity.
        Mozart was born in 1756.
        Lewis Carroll (*Alice in Wonderland*) was born in 1832.
        In 1906 the River Thames caught fire as oil on the surface ignited.
        In 1926 the first TV pictures were demonstrated in London by John Logie Baird.

28th   Henry VII died in 1547.

Francis Drake died in 1596 on his ship off the coast of Panama.

In 1807 London's Pall Mall became the first street in the world to be lit by gaslight.

In 1986 the American space shuttle *Challenger* exploded on lift-off, killing its crew of seven.

29th St Francis's Day. He is the patron saint of writers and journalists. He died in 1662 and is known fully as St Francis de Sales.

The Victoria Cross was first awarded on this day in 1856. The medals were made from guns captured in the Crimea.

In 1947 one of the coldest ever spells of winter weather in Britain saw temperatures at −16°F. (*Link – Assemblies 10 and 11*)

30th King Charles I was beheaded in 1649.

Edward Lear, poet, died in 1888.

Mahatma Gandhi was assassinated in New Delhi, India, in 1948. 'Mahatma' means 'Great Soul'.

In 1958 a bill was passed in the House of Lords marking lifetime peerages for men and women. For the first time in over six centuries women were admitted to the House of Lords.

31st Guy Fawkes was executed in 1606.

While on the subject of 'bonfires', on this night in 1804, with the country apprehensive about a French invasion, a warning bonfire was accidentally set alight near Berwick. This triggered off the lighting of many others and by morning all the southern Scottish counties were armed and ready to fight.

In one year, up to this date in 1922, the cost of living in Germany had risen by 73.7%.

Car front-seatbelts became compulsory in the UK in 1983.

Religious notes

Epiphany is the Christian feast which occurs twelve days after Christmas. It was originally associated with the baptism of Christ. An interesting link with the traditional story of the three wise men and their gifts is that these same gifts are presented at the altar in St James Palace, Chapel Royal, by members of the British royal family at this time of year.

January 25th has already been mentioned in the foregoing notes as St Paul's Day. It has another significance in that the week of prayer for Christian Unity is timed to end on this day.

The Hindu festival of Vasanta Panchami takes place in the month of Magha (January/February) and is a celebration of Sarasvati who is the goddess of learning and wisdom.

February

February (along with January) was one of the two months by which Numa Pompilius extended the Roman year from ten to twelve periods. The name came from the word 'februare', meaning 'to purify'.

1st   This is St Bride's Day. She is the patroness of Ireland.

       In 1811 the beacon on Bell Rock lighthouse was first lit. In earlier times the Abbot of Aberbrothock had put a bell on this rock, off the Firth of Tay, to warn mariners of its presence. A pirate called Ralph the Rover cut this bell adrift and sent it into the sea. Later his ship was wrecked on the same rock and he was drowned. (Junior children find this a very telling story!) (*Link – Assembly 47*)

       In 1915 passport photographs were first introduced in Great Britain.

       In the same year, Sir Stanley Matthews, possibly England's most famous ever footballer, was born. He played until he was fifty.

2nd   Candlemas. On this date many churches have candlelit processions to celebrate the presentation of Jesus in the temple. In former times candles were thought of as 'representations' of the all-important sun, and were considered a talisman against such dreads as famine and plague. One other reason for the Church's emphasis on candles was to counteract these pagan celebrations. Candles and light symbolise good, truth, knowledge, hope and an early reference to Jesus the child said that he was 'a light to lighten the Gentiles' (Luke 2, 32). Candlemas Day is another of those which has traditional weather lore attached to it:

> 'If Candlemas Day be fair and bright,
> Winter will have another flight;
> But if it be dark with clouds and rain,
> Winter is gone and will not come again.'

       Tradition also names the snowdrop as the flower for 2nd February. It is said to have been created from a snowflake by an angel to give Adam and Eve hope when they had been expelled from the Garden of Eden. (*Link – Assembly 21*)

3rd In Japan this is seen as the last day of winter and, to celebrate, people throw beans at each other. (*Link – Class Assembly 2*)

Felix Mendelssohn was born in 1809.

This is the feast day of St Blaise, a saint with the power to cure throat problems.

On this day in 1953 hurricanes and high tides brought disaster to Britain's east coast. Two hundred and fifty people were drowned and thousands were made homeless. (*Link – Assemblies 11 and 47*)

4th Charles Lindbergh, the first man to fly solo over the Atlantic, was born in 1902. (*Link – Assembly 51*)

In 1929 the first Green Belt area round London was approved. This was a five-mile tract near Hendon.

On this date in 1953 sweet rationing ended in Great Britain.

5th St Agatha's Day. Agatha was being tortured for being a Christian when an earthquake erupted. It stopped when her torture stopped. She died peacefully in 251 AD.

Robert Peel, founder of the British police force, was born in 1788. (*Link – Class Assembly 1*)

The *Reader's Digest* was first published in 1922.

In 1983 an unknown Mozart symphony was found among a pile of old papers in Odense, Denmark. It was calculated that the composer had written it when he was nine years old.

6th On this day in 1918 the Representation of the People Act came into force, allowing women to vote in General Elections. They had to be over thirty, and householders. (Equal voting rights for all adults were won in 1928.)

In 1927 a ten-year-old boy in short trousers made a sensational debut playing the violin at a concert in Paris. His name was Yehudi Menuhin.

In 1958 the Manchester United football team's aeroplane crashed in Munich following a European cup tie. Seven of the players died immediately.

In 1964 Britain and France agreed to build a Channel Tunnel.

7th Charles Dickens was born in 1812.

This was the day, in 1845, when William Lloyd went into the British Museum and deliberately broke the priceless 300-year-old Portland Vase, which had been discovered in Rome.

He was fined for the vandalism. The vase, shattered into 2,000 pieces, was laboriously repaired by a man called Doubleday. (*Link – Assembly 42*)

On this date in 1960 Israeli archaeologists discovered some parchment scrolls containing Biblical texts. The scrolls were estimated as having been written 1,700 years ago.

8th   Jules Verne, the author of *Around the World in Eighty Days*, was born in 1823.

9th   St Apollonia's Day. During her torture for being a Christian, in Alexandria, Apollonia's teeth were removed to make her renounce her faith, which she would not do. She died in 249 AD and is the patron saint of dentists.

This was the date in 1855 when, after a fall of snow in south-west England, mysterious footprints appeared next morning. These ran for nearly one hundred miles – over roofs and haystacks. They were cloven hooves – the mystery was never solved. (*Link – Assembly 56*)

After eighteen days of continuous rain, London suburbs started to flood on this date in 1926.

In 1939 the British Government announced that London families on an income of less than £250 a year would be given free air-raid shelters.

10th   St Scholastica's Day. Scholastica died in 543. She was the sister of the better-known St Benedict who founded the Benedictine monastery at Monte Cassino in Italy.

Samuel Plimsoll was born in 1824. (*Link – Assembly 24*)

This was the date, in 1913, when rescuers found the dead bodies of Captain Scott and his two companions in their snow-covered tent near the South Pole. Scott's diary was found with them.

On this date in 1942 the first Golden Disc for a successful recording was presented. It was to Glenn Miller and his band for their hit, 'Chattanooga Choo Choo'.

11th   This is a day of celebration in Japan – to commemorate the founding of the country in 660 BC.

12th   Alexander Selkirk (the model for Defoe's Robinson Crusoe) was rescued from the uninhabited island of Juan Fernandez on this day in 1709. He had been there alone for five years.

Abraham Lincoln, sixteenth president of the United States, was born in 1809. He was responsible for the emancipation of negro slaves after the Civil War. He made the famous Gettysburg Address: 'This nation, under God, shall have a new birth of freedom; and that government of the people, by the people, and for the people, shall not perish from the earth.'

13th   On this date in 1978 Anna Ford became ITV's first female newscaster.

14th   St Valentine's Day. In the third century the Roman Emperor Claudius II passed a law against marriage because it was denuding his army of troops. A Christian priest, Valentine, continued to marry couples. He was discovered and sentenced to death. His compassion for all – including his jailer and that man's daughter – earned him sainthood. The sending of Valentine cards was probably at its peak in Britain in the nineteenth century. Postmen in London at this time felt that their task was so onerous on this day that they asked for a special meal allowance. (*Link – Assembly 26*)

15th   Galileo Galilei, the astronomer, was born in 1564.
       Decimal currency was introduced in Britain in 1971.

16th   Desperate unemployment in Britain in 1921 included 368,000 ex-servicemen.
       Tutenkhamen's tomb and contents were discovered in Egypt in 1923.
       The new synthetic fibre, nylon, was patented in New York on this date in 1937. Its name came from the two cities where work on its development had taken place: NY (New York) and LON (London).

17th   Michaelangelo Buonarotti, the Italian artist who decorated the ceiling of the Sistine Chapel, died in 1563.
       In 1920 Britain's police force started to replace its horses with cars.

18th   St Simon, Bishop of Jerusalem, nephew of Joseph and Mary and Christ's cousin, was crucified in 116. He was 120 years old.
       Martin Luther died in 1546.
       A new planet was sighted and named in 1930 – Pluto.
       In 1942, to save fuel and soap during the Second World War, people in Britain were urged to take fewer baths, and to paint a 'plimsoll line' in bathtubs to regulate the amount of water put into them.
       In 1949 the millionth ton of airlifted supplies reached the western sector of the beleaguered Berlin.

19th   Nicholas Copernicus, the astronomer, was born in 1473.

20th   Traditionally, old almanacs recommended this date as the date to sow beans. In folklore the bean is associated with ghosts and witches. In days when witches were feared it was recommended that lonely travellers carried a bean in their mouths to spit at a witch if one appeared.

Jimmy Greaves, the international footballer, was born in 1940.

21st   Cardinal Newman, who wrote the hymn 'Lead, kindly light', was born in London in 1801.

In 1842 John Greenough received a patent for the sewing machine.

In 1956 the Duke of Edinburgh announced an award scheme for enterprising young people. (*Link – Assembly 28; Class Assembly 1*)

22nd   The first Woolworth's store opened in New York in 1879.

In 1910 X-ray machines were first used in medical treatment.

23rd   Samuel Pepys, the diarist, was born in 1632.

George Frederick Handel was born in 1685.

Dame Nellie Melba, the singer who had the 'peach melba' named after her, died in 1931. (*Link – Assembly 44*)

In 1975, Laurence Stephen Lowry, the artist, died. He was born in 1887.

24th   This is the feast day of St Matthias. Matthias was the apostle who took the place of Judas Iscariot after the latter committed suicide. (Bible ref: Acts 1, 23–26)

Wilhelm Karl Grimm (of the Grimm brothers' fairy tales) was born in 1786.

25th   Sir Christopher Wren, the architect, died in 1723.

So important to Naples and Italy was the great opera singer, Enrico Caruso, born this day in 1873, that the world's largest candle was dedicated to his memory. It was eighteen feet high when new and is lit every year on his birthday. It is expected to last for 1,800 years. (*Link – Assembly 44*)

26th   Victor Hugo (author of *Les Misérables*, which contains the story of the Bishop's candlesticks, such a good assembly tale) was born in 1846.

27th   This day celebrates St Thalilaeus who died in the fifth century. He is remembered for his constant weeping as penance for his sins.

In 1964 engineers in Italy pronounced the leaning tower of Pisa dangerous. They said it needed straightening by eleven feet to stop it falling over.

28th   In 1912 the first parachute jump from a plane was made by Albert Berry in Missouri, USA.

       In 1975 the driver and thirty-five passengers died in a London Underground train disaster at Moorgate. (*Link – Assembly 45*)

29th   The Leap Year tradition of women asking men to marry them was once taken so seriously in Scotland that a law was passed saying that any man who turned down such a proposal would be heavily fined.

Religious notes

Candlemas, on 2nd February, celebrates Jesus's presentation at the temple. At the time Jesus was born it was customary for every Jewish mother to go to the temple forty days after the birth of her first male child so that he could be 'presented to the Lord'. The mother was also 'blessed' on this occasion. Candles have come to celebrate this day in connection with Jesus being 'the light of the world'.

    Lent is the period from Ash Wednesday to Holy Saturday – forty weekdays. During this time Christians remember the temptations of Jesus in the wilderness. It is a time for spiritual preparation for Easter.

    The fact that the Muslim calendar is based on the lunar year makes it impossible to give notable Muslim dates fixed locations in a book like this, but in 1993, 1994 and 1995 the month of Ramadan begins in February. During Ramadan Muslims refrain from eating and drinking (also smoking and conjugal relations) between dawn and sunset. This annual fasting (*saum*) is one of the five essential Islamic practices and is designed to raise moral and spiritual standards, and as a means of self-control.

    During the last ten days of Ramadan Muslims celebrate the festival of Lailat-ul-Qadr. This is Arabic for 'The Night of Power' for it was on this night that the Holy Qur'an was revealed to the Prophet Muhammad by the Archangel Gabriel.

March

The word 'March' comes from the Roman 'Martius'. It was originally the first month of the Roman calendar, named after the God of War.

1st   St David's Day. The emblem of the leek originated from soldiers wearing them in their hats to distinguish them from the Saxon enemy in battle. A great victory was won on this day and is commemorated by the same emblem.

In Switzerland cow bells 'ring out winter' on this date.

In 1976 a Road Traffic Bill was approved in the British Parliament. Its aim was to make the wearing of car seatbelts compulsory.

2nd   John Wesley, the founder of Methodism, died in 1791.

This is the feast of St Chad, a Christian missionary.

Mikhail Gorbachev was born in 1931.

In 1949 on this date the US airforce B-50 Superfortress *Lucky Lady II* completed the first non-stop flight round the world – 23,452 miles.

3rd   Alexander Graham Bell, inventor of the telephone, was born in 1847.

Fatima Whitbread, the javelin thrower, was born in 1961.

In 1937 on this date it was announced that Britain had 824 millionaires. (*Link – Assembly 4*)

In 1955 notice was given that London would be a 'smokeless zone' from October onwards.

In 1958 the first parking tickets were issued to British motorists.

4th   In 1824 the Royal National Lifeboat Institution was founded. (*Link – Assembly 24*)

Concern was expressed in Britain in 1873 at the fact that, on average, 2,754 merchant seamen lost their lives every year.

In 1927, 25,000 diggers rushed to stake their claims in the new South African diamond fields. (*Link – Assembly 4*)

In 1982 London's Barbican Centre was opened by the Queen.

5th   The Spitfire made its maiden flight in 1936. It was flown from Eastleigh Airport, Southampton, by Captain J Summers.

In 1942, in an effort to save pencils during wartime economies, all civil servants had their pencil sharpeners withdrawn.

6th   Davy Crockett and 86 others died when Mexican forces captured Fort Alamo in 1836.

This is the birthday of Sri Ramakrishna, the Hindu teacher, in 1833.

In 1946, when Great Britain was still suffering from food shortages, the British food ministry issued a recipe for squirrel pie. (*Link – Assembly 16*)

On this date in 1947 Britain continued to suffer one of its

worst ever winters when three hundred roads were blocked and fifteen towns cut off. (*Link – Assembly 10*)

In 1987 the *Herald of Free Enterprise*, a Townsend Thoresen car ferry, capsized off the Belgian port of Zeebrugge at 7pm when it was setting out for Dover. It happened so quickly that there was no time to send an SOS and 193 people lost their lives. (*Link – Assembly 24*)

7th   The British and Foreign Bible Society was founded in 1804. It has been responsible for translations into over 1,500 different languages. (*Link – Class Assemblies 3 and 4*)

St Perpetua's Day. She was martyred in 203 AD when she died before a crowd of thousands in the Rome amphitheatre.

The Albert Medal, for gallantry in saving life, was instituted in 1866.

In 1965 traffic jams blocked roads round Regent's Park, London, where crowds gathered to watch Goldie, a golden eagle who had escaped from London Zoo. He was recaptured on the 10th.

In 1969 the Queen opened the new London Underground line from Victoria to Walthamstow. (*Link – Assembly 45*)

8th   International Women's Day.

In 1834 a Newfoundland dog called Hero saved two boys from drowning in the River Thames. As a result ten Newfoundlands were bought and trained for similar life-saving duties along the Seine in Paris. (*Link – Assemblies 38 and 57*)

The first British pilot's licence was issued in 1910. (*Link – Assembly 51*)

On this date in 1906 the British Empire occupied one fifth of the land surface of the globe and had a population of four hundred million.

In 1925 the 'crossword craze' brought forth conflicting comments. The British Optical Association feared they would cause eye strain and headaches; the Chicago Department of Health announced that their mental stimulation was good for health and happiness. (*Link – Assemblies 30 and 41*)

9th   C M Howard invented false teeth in 1827.

The French Foreign Legion was founded in 1831.

10th   The first Cruft's Dog Show was held in London in 1886. (*Link – Assemblies 14, 20, 38 and 57*)

Harriet Tubman died in 1913. She was famous for her work in helping slaves to escape during the American Civil War.

The first 'movie' was made in Hollywood in 1910. It was called *In Old California*.

11th   Johnny Appleseed, the famous American apple tree planter, died in 1847.

Sir Alexander Fleming, discoverer of penicillin, died in 1955.

In 1985 Mikhail Gorbachev became the new leader of the USSR.

12th   This is the feast day of St Gregory the Great, who sent St Augustine on his mission to England in 597.

In 1908 Benjamin Waugh, founder of the NSPCC, died. (*Link – Assembly 3*)

Coins replaced English £1 notes in 1983.

13th   From this day onwards in 1886 British soldiers were allowed to wear beards.

The discovery of the planet Pluto was announced in 1930.

In 1918 the British school-leaving age was raised to fourteen.

14th   Albert Einstein, the physicist, was born in 1879.

In 1934 it was announced that eggs in Britain had dropped to their lowest price since 1914 – 6d (2½p) per dozen.

15th   Julius Caesar, Roman Emperor, was murdered in 44 BC.

The first cricket Test match was played between Australia and England at Melbourne, Australia. The Australians won by 45 runs.

In 1909 Selfridges opened in London's Oxford Street.

In 1949 clothes rationing (which had been introduced in Britain in 1941) ended.

16th   The first English FA Cup Final took place in 1872. (Wanderers beat the Royal Engineers.)

In 1917 the Czar abdicated in the face of the Russian Revolution.

In 1919 the invention of the wireless telephone enabled air pilots to talk in flight. (*Link – Assembly 51*)

In 1912, Lawrence Oates, thinking his death would aid the survival of his four colleagues, left the tent of Captain Scott's South Pole expedition, and walked in the snow to his death. (*Link – Assembly 57*)

17th   St Patrick's Day. Patrick died in 464. He was sent to Ireland by Pope Celestine to convert the heathens there. One of the ways in which he did this was to show them a shamrock –

where three leaves combine to make a single plant. This he linked to the Trinity and the shamrock became a national emblem.

Feast day of St Joseph of Arimathea – who placed the body of Jesus in the tomb. (*Link – Class Assembly 4*)

18th   John Luther Jones ('Casey Jones') stayed at the controls of his runaway train on the Chicago–New Orleans Line and died saving as many lives as he could when the train crashed. This was in 1900. The famous ballad recalls his story. (*Link – Assembly 45*)

In 1945 all schools and universities were closed in Tokyo. Everyone over six years old was ordered to do war work.

19th   This is the feast day of St Joseph, Mary's husband.

Sydney Harbour Bridge was opened in 1932.

In 1962, the discovery of a 300-year-old skull was made beneath 10 Downing Street.

In 1964 the St Bernard Tunnel between Switzerland and Italy, via the Alps, was opened.

In 1967 an oil tanker, the *Torrey Canyon*, ran aground at Land's End and its cargo of oil began spilling into the sea. RAF planes later bombed it to disperse the oil which was said to be the 'greatest peacetime threat to Britain'.

20th   Sir Isaac Newton died in 1727.

In 1967 Sir Francis Chichester began the last leg of his solo voyage round the world.

21st   Feast of St Benedict. As Abbot of the monastery at Monte Cassino, he founded the order of Benedictine monks.

Johann Sebastian Bach was born in 1685.

22nd   Johann Wolfgang von Goethe, the German philosopher, died in 1832. He was so clever that he could speak French, Italian, Latin and Greek by the time he was eight years old.

The English Football League was founded with twelve clubs in 1888.

23rd   Roger Bannister, the first man to run a mile in under four minutes, was born in 1929.

24th   Queen Elizabeth I died in 1603 after reigning for 44 years.

25th   Lady Day, Feast of the Annunciation of the Virgin Mary. (Luke 1, 26–38)

Opening of London Airport, Heathrow, in 1948.

Some old English tombstones show interesting inscriptions which concern this date. In the graveyard of the parish church of St Mary, North Mymms, Hertfordshire, the tombstone of Thomas Huxley puts his death in 1695/6. This signifies the fact that until 1752 the legal New Year in Britain began on 25th March; the 'popular' New Year was 1st January. Consequently it was not unusual for gravestones recording deaths between 1st January and 24th March to show both years.

26th   Ludwig van Beethoven died in 1827.

The first BBC weather forecast was broadcast on this date in 1923.

27th   The first international wireless message was sent by Marconi in 1899.

Yuri Gagarin, the Soviet cosmonaut, died in 1968.

28th   The first European use of gunpowder was at a battle between Venetians and Genoese in 1380.

The Crimean War began in 1854.

29th   The actress Sarah Bernhardt died, aged 78, on this day in 1923. (Traffic came to a halt in Paris for her funeral.)

In 1981 Dick Beardsley of the USA won the first London Marathon.

30th   Anna Sewell, the author of *Black Beauty*, was born in 1820. (*Link – Assembly 50*)

Vincent van Gogh, the artist, was born on this date in 1853. His painting 'Sunflowers' was sold at Christie's in London for £24,750,000 in 1987. (*Link – Assembly 4*)

31st   The Eiffel Tower was opened in Paris in 1889. It is 300 metres high but was not universally popular – over a hundred leading French writers, artists and composers claimed it was an affront to French taste and architecture.

In 1911 it was announced in Britain that the Government was seeking to make sixty hours the maximum working time for shop workers. (*Link – Assembly 48*)

Religious notes

Purim is the Jewish festival which celebrates how the Jews of Persia were saved from the persecution of Haman. Because he hated the wise Mordecai, Haman and his followers planned a wholesale slaughter of the Jews throughout the kingdom. His plans were foiled when Esther, Mordecai's niece, was chosen by King Ahasuerus as his new queen. She revealed Haman's plot to the king. Modern celebrations at this festival are light-hearted and jolly. Much fancy dress is worn and hisses and noises greet Haman's name whenever it is mentioned. (*Link – Assembly 43*)

The same aura of colour, spectacle and jollity pervades the Hindu spring festival of Holi. On the first day of the festival a bonfire is lit, and on the second day people throw coloured water and powder over each other and exchange presents. These activities celebrate the revels of Lord Krishna. (*Link – Class Assembly 2*)

In 1993, 1994 and 1995, the Muslim festival of Eid-ul-Fitr occurs in March too. Here again it is a festival of joy as it celebrates the end of the month-long fast of Ramadan.

April

Few months make such an initial impact with their first day as does April! It is also a time for obvious, and sage, advice: 'April showers bring May flowers' (*Link – Assembly 55*); and ' 'Til April's dead, change not a thread.'

1st   An attempt to trace the origins of April Fools' Day is confused by its popularity in France, where an April Fools' trick is an 'April Fish' (*'un poisson d'avril'*), and by the similar goings-on at the Hindu Holi celebrations. One suggestion is that when New Year's Day used to be 25th March, 1st April presented itself as a day of levity to end the celebrations.

The Royal Air Force was founded in 1918.

2nd   Hans Andersen was born in 1805. Two of his tales which are useful for assemblies are 'The Ugly Duckling' and 'The Emperor's New Clothes'. Appropriately enough, this is also International Children's Book Day. (*Link – Assembly 53*)

3rd   The Pony Express was founded on this date in 1860 when two riders set out in the USA. One was going east from San Francisco, the other west from St Joseph, Missouri. During its short life, 80 riders and 500 horses worked on the 1,900 miles of the organisation's route. (*Link – Assembly 50*)

4th   St Ambrose died on this date in 397. A great orator, he is credited with the famous phrase: 'When you are in Rome, do as they do in Rome.'

Martin Luther King, the American civil rights leader, was assassinated in Memphis in 1968. A few days later (on 9th April) over 150,000 people attended his burial in Atlanta.

5th   Robert Raikes died in 1811. He founded Sunday Schools for children throughout Britain. His first school was opened in 1780 in Gloucester, and was for poor children. (*Link – Assembly 29*)

On this date in 1955 Sir Winston Churchill resigned as Prime Minister at the age of eighty.

6th   Albrecht Dürer, the artist ('Praying Hands') died in 1528.

Houdini, the great escape artist, was born in 1874.

Robert Edwin Peary became the first man to reach the North Pole in 1909. He and his party had set out from New York by ship in July 1908.

7th   The highwayman Dick Turpin was hanged in York in 1739.

In 1832, at Carlisle, Joseph Thomson sold his wife to Henry Mears for twenty shillings and a dog.

This is World Health Day, when prayers are asked for sick and suffering people all over the world.

8th   This is the date of a Mahayana Buddhist celebration of Buddha Sakyamuni's birthday.

9th   Isambard Kingdom Brunel, the engineer, was born in 1806.

The American Civil War ended in 1865.

A letter appeared in *The Times* of London asking for a new word to describe 'progress by electric power'. Eventually the word 'motor' was chosen.

10th   William Booth, co-founder, with his wife Catherine, of the Salvation Army, was born in 1829. (Salvation Army, 101 Queen Victoria Street, London EC4P 4EP) (*Link – Assembly 29*)

The *Titanic*, the world's largest ship, set off on its ill-fated maiden voyage from Southampton to New York on this date in 1912.

11th   St Guthlac, who died in 714, renounced his earlier career as a robber, took to living in a swamp in the English Fens and existed on only bread and water for the rest of his life.

Napoleon was exiled to Elba in 1814.

12th   The American Civil War broke out in 1861.

The Russian cosmonaut, Yuri Alekseyerich Gagarin, made the first manned space flight round the earth. His space craft was called *Vostok* and the orbit took 89 minutes.

13th   This is the date of Baisakhi, the festival which commemorates the founding of the Sikh Kalsa (brotherhood) by Guru Gobind Singh in 1699. The five symbols of the religion worn by the Kalsa are: the *kesh* (uncut hair), the *kanga* (a comb to hold hair under the turban); the *kara* (a bracelet), the *kirpan* (a sword), and the *kaccha* (shorts).

14th   Traditionally this is the date on which the cuckoo is first heard in Britain.

Abraham Lincoln, US President, was shot by John Wilkes Booth in 1865. Booth was later killed resisting arrest.

15th   Leonardo da Vinci was born in 1452.

This is traditionally Swallow Day in Britain – when swallows return for the spring and summer.

Father Damien, who gave his life treating lepers, was born in 1889.

The *Titanic* sank after hitting an iceberg in 1912 and 1,513 people were drowned.

In 1989 ninety-four people died at the Hillsborough football stadium disaster in Sheffield.

Religious notes

The Sikh festival of Baisakhi takes place on 13th April (see the note for this date).

Although it is a movable feast, Easter often occurs in this month. The build-up to Easter is considerable. Lent is preceded by Shrove Tuesday when worshippers went to church to be 'shriven' – confess their sins. Ash Wednesday, as the first day of Lent, is a time when Christians daubed ash on their faces as a further reminder of the need to repent sins. The forty days of Lent then follow, as a spiritual preparation for Easter. It should be remembered that these forty days do not include Sundays – which always remain feast days, not fast days. Holy Week precedes Easter Sunday, which is the joyous celebration of Jesus's resurrection and which activates thoughts through the next forty days to Ascension Day. (*Link – Class Assemblies 3 and 4*)

The Jewish Pesach (Passover) festival is held to celebrate the escape of the Children of Israel from Egypt. This happened under the leadership of Moses, more than three thousand years ago. Passover occurs in the Jewish month of Nisan and lasts for eight days – the first two and the last two are full festival days.

The house is thoroughly cleaned and a meal prepared. No leaven (yeast) must be used. On the first evening of the festival, the family, dressed in their best (or new) clothes, come to the table for the Seder. Each member of the family has a cup of wine and certain food (bitter herbs, a lamb's shank bone, a roasted egg, a mixture of apples and nuts in a paste, watercress and unleavened bread). These foods are symbolic. Exodus 12 tells the story of the Passover. (*Link – Class Assembly 5*)

Section D
Assemblies linked by theme

This section seeks to aid teachers who wish to present a number of assemblies linked by themes which are popular ones in a primary school and RE context. No assembly story from the book has been used more than three times in the groupings which follow. The assemblies are shown by their numbers and title.

Animals

1   This month (January)
21 This month (February)
37 This month (March)
55 This month (April)
2   The hero
5   A helping paw
14 A dog's life
18 The recipe
20 Judy
25 We need a king!
30 A great discovery
32 Winkie
36 More!
38 One hot Australian day
46 The lost sheep
49 Hero Wong
50 What is your opinion?
57 Ruswarp the faithful

Concern

3   Home Sweet Home?
9   Here he comes
11 It will be all right
14 A dog's life
15 Peace and quiet
17 Is it worth it?
28 Teamwork
31 In a garden in Medina
35 Guard my treasure
42 A cause for concern
50 What is your opinion?
56 Mother Samwell

Courage

10 Avalanche!
24 Rescue
28 Teamwork
30 A great discovery
32 Winkie
33 Doing what is best
45 Thanks, driver!
47 The Ethel Langton story
49 Hero Wong
51 I need some help
58 Don't leave it too late

Environment

1   This month (January)
21 This month (February)
37 This month (March)
55 This month (April)
3   Home Sweet Home?

12 The cut
15 Peace and quiet
16 Our daily bread
23 Pass it on
40 Not quite perfect
42 A cause for concern
48 All change
52 A good joke
54 Is that really what you want?

Class assemblies

1 The best time is now
3 What was it like?

Faith

8 St Nathalan
9 Here he comes
27 The plot
31 In a garden in Medina
33 Doing what is best
39 Tell the truth
41 The healing of the blind man
43 The idols
46 The lost sheep

Class assemblies:

2 Fun for all
4 Report from Jerusalem
5 Food for thought

Friendship

5 A helping paw
7 The weekend
10 Avalanche!
23 Pass it on
28 Teamwork
34 Welcome to a stranger
38 One hot Australian day
52 A good joke

Class assembly:

1 The best time is now

Guidance

4 Good value?
6 The prince
9 Here he comes
13 Be prepared
25 We need a king!
26 Two's company
29 The man whom everybody
    liked
30 A great discovery
48 All change
51 I need some help
58 Don't leave it too late
59 Learning a lesson

Heroes and heroines

2 The hero
24 Rescue
32 Winkie
44 Fame
45 Thanks, driver!
47 The Ethel Langton story
49 Hero Wong
51 I need some help

Home

3 Home Sweet Home?
7 The weekend
12 The cut
18 The recipe
26 Two's company
29 The man whom everybody
    liked
34 Welcome to a stranger

Class assembly:

5   Food for thought

Journeys

6   The prince
8   St Nathalan
13   Be prepared
19   What's inside?
31   In a garden in Medina
34   Welcome to a stranger
38   One hot Australian day
50   What is your opinion?

Living together

12   The cut
13   Be prepared
15   Peace and quiet
23   Pass it on
25   We need a king!
26   Two's company
33   Doing what is best
40   Not quite perfect
54   Is that really what you want?
56   Mother Samwell

Class assemblies:

2   Fun for all
5   Food for thought

Ourselves

4   Good value?

22   Patience
23   Pass it on
40   Not quite perfect
48   All change
58   Don't leave it too late
59   Learning a lesson
60   Don't count your chickens
     before they're hatched

Senses

1   This month (January)
21   This month (February)
37   This month (March)
55   This month (April)
16   Our daily bread
41   The healing of the blind man

Class assembly:

2   Fun for all

Those who help us

10   Avalanche!
12   The cut
18   The recipe
24   Rescue
29   The man whom everybody
     liked
45   Thanks, driver!
46   The lost sheep

Section E
The stories

This section classifies the stories according to source categories – *folk, true, religious, original or contemporary* – for teachers who wish to use them in groupings of this nature. The assemblies are shown by their numbers and titles.

Folk stories, myths, legends

2   The hero
5   A helping paw
6   The prince
18 The recipe
22 Patience
25 We need a king!
26 Two's company
34 Welcome to a stranger
35 Guard my treasure
36 More!
39 Tell the truth
54 Is that really what you want?
59 Learning a lesson

True stories

1   This month (January)
3   Home Sweet Home?
7   The weekend
10 Avalanche!
11 It will be all right
12 The cut
14 A dog's life
16 Our daily bread
17 Is it worth it?
19 What's inside?
20 Judy
21 This month (February)
24 Rescue

28 Teamwork
29 The man whom everybody liked
30 A great discovery
32 Winkie
37 This month (March)
38 One hot Australian day
40 Not quite perfect
42 A cause for concern
44 Fame
45 Thanks, driver!
47 The Ethel Langton story
49 Hero Wong
50 What is your opinion?
51 I need some help
52 A good joke
53 The second chance
55 This month (April)
56 Mother Samwell
57 Ruswarp the faithful
58 Don't leave it too late

Class assembly:

1   The best time is now

Religious stories

4   Good value?
8   St Nathalan
9   Here he comes

13   Be prepared
27   The plot
31   In a garden in Medina
33   Doing what is best
41   The healing of the blind man
43   The idols
46   The lost sheep

Class assemblies:

2   Fun for all
3   What was it like?

4   Report from Jerusalem
5   Food for thought

Original or contemporary stories

15   Peace and quiet
23   Pass it on
48   All change
60   Don't count your chickens
     before they're hatched

Section F
National Curriculum
cross-references

This section is intended as a guide for teachers who wish to integrate these assemblies into other areas of the National Curriculum. The assemblies are shown by their number and title, listed under the appropriate subject heading (subjects in alphabetical order).

Art

11 It will be all right
21 This month (February)
25 We need a king!
26 Two's company
31 In a garden in Medina
37 This month (March)
40 Not quite perfect

Class assemblies:
2   Fun for all
4   Report from Jerusalem

English

All the stories in this book could be incorporated into some aspect of English work – discussion, drama, expressing opinions, writing creatively and descriptively.

Geography

2   The hero
4   Good value?

8   St Nathalan
9   Here he comes
10 Avalanche!
11 It will be all right
12 The cut
17 Is it worth it?
19 What's inside?
21 This month (February)
22 Patience
24 Rescue
27 The plot
28 Teamwork
29 The man whom everybody liked
31 In a garden in Medina
38 One hot Australian day
40 Not quite perfect
41 The healing of the blind man
44 Fame
46 The lost sheep
47 The Ethel Langton story
49 Hero Wong
54 Is that really what you want?
57 Ruswarp the faithful

History

1 This month (January)
4 Good value?
6 The prince
8 St Nathalan
9 Here he comes
12 The cut
13 Be prepared
16 Our daily bread
17 Is it worth it?
19 What's inside?
21 This month (February)
24 Rescue
29 The man whom everybody liked
31 In a garden in Medina
34 Welcome to a stranger
40 Not quite perfect
42 A cause for concern
43 The idols
46 The lost sheep
47 The Ethel Langton story
48 All change
50 What is your opinion?
55 This month (April)
56 Mother Samwell
57 Ruswarp the faithful
58 Don't leave it too late

Mathematics

4 Good value?
29 The man whom everybody liked
32 Winkie
45 Thanks, driver!

Music

2 The hero
23 Pass it on
24 Rescue

26 Two's company
37 This month (March)
43 The idols
44 Fame
46 The lost sheep
52 A good joke
54 Is that really what you want?
55 This month (April)
60 Don't count your chickens before they're hatched

Class assembly:
5 Food for thought

Physical education

2 The hero
28 Teamwork

Science

1 This month (January)
2 The hero
5 A helping paw
8 St Nathalan
10 Avalanche!
11 It will be all right
12 The cut
13 Be prepared
14 A dog's life
15 Peace and quiet
16 Our daily bread
17 Is it worth it?
19 What's inside?
20 Judy
21 This month (February)
22 Patience
24 Rescue
28 Teamwork
30 A great discovery
32 Winkie
36 More!
37 This month (March)

39 Tell the truth
41 The healing of the blind man
45 Thanks, driver!
46 The lost sheep
47 The Ethel Langton story
50 What is your opinion?
51 I need some help
54 Is that really what you want?
55 This month (April)
57 Ruswarp the faithful
59 Learning a lesson
60 Don't count your chickens before they're hatched

Technology

12 The cut
17 Is it worth it?

19 What's inside?
20 Judy
22 Patience
24 Rescue
28 Teamwork
30 A great discovery
31 In a garden in Medina
33 Doing what is best
35 Guard my treasure
36 More!
47 The Ethel Langton story
48 All change
57 Ruswarp the faithful
59 Learning a lesson

Class assembly:

5 Food for thought

Section G

Resources

Addresses

SAEs are welcomed when you contact the following addresses, which are useful for specially produced material.

General

Save the Children, Mary Datchelor House, 17 Grove Lane, London SE5 8SP. (The magazines are a constant source of excellent assembly stories.)

The RE Centre, National Society (Church of England) for Promoting Religious Education, 23 Kensington Square, London W8 5HN. The Centre distributes the annual journal of the SHAP Working Party on World Religions in Education, which is particularly valuable for precise annual dates of religious festivals.

SHAP teachers' information service: Vida Barnett, 81 St Mary's Road, Huyton, Merseyside L36 5SR.

Independent Publishing Company, 38 Kennington Lane, London SE11 4LS. They publish a large selection of books, posters and cards relating particularly to South-East Asian countries.

Christianity

Christian Education Movement, Royal Buildings, Victoria Street, Derby DE1 1GW. By subscribing to the CEM schools receive a termly mailing of material which is always useful for RE, and sometimes specially aimed at assemblies.

Hinduism

Hindu Centre, 7 Cedars Road, London E15 4NE.

ISCON Educational Services, Bhakti Vedanta Manor, Letchworth, Hertfordshire WD2 8ED.

Islam

Iqra Trust, 24 Culross Street, London W1Y 3HE.

Muslim Educational Trust, 130 Stroud Green Road, London N4 3RZ.

Judaism
Jewish Education Bureau, 8 Westcombe Avenue, Leeds L58 2BS.

Books and stories

One of the difficulties of recommending books is that, particularly in recent years, titles have either gone out of print or changed publishers at a bewildering rate.

The wise teacher therefore will seek to build up a range in two areas. The first of these would be the background-information type of book, including material like *Celebrations*, a series of booklets by Maurice Lynch (Ginn). Other most useful sources are: *Festival*, a series of booklets by Olivia Bennett (Commonwealth Institute and Macmillan); *Festivals and Saints' Days* by V Green (Blandford); Black's *Bible Dictionary* (A C Black).

The second collection will consist of folk tales which often produce marvellous assembly material. New anthologies appear with great regularity and should always be examined carefully. Old favourites like *Anansi*, the *Hodja*, *Brer Rabbit* and Aesop's *Fables* are suitable for many re-tellings and adaptations.

A very good way to find out about new and useful books in this field is to subscribe to *Books for Keeps*, a magazine of children's books (6 Brightfield Road, London SE12 8QF).

A book of anniversaries is always useful. The *Longman History of the 20th Century* is a marvellous source. It is usually 'for reference only' in public libraries but is an invaluable addition to any school's reference library.

Newspapers provide an endless supply of stimulating true stories, and the advantage of local newspapers is that they often have appropriate stories which have taken place in settings familiar to the children.

Teachers should not neglect Asian-owned newsagencies either. These are useful sources for items such as festival cards and Hindu legends in comic-strip form.

Resources for music

The BBC's *Come and Praise* anthologies are the source for all the hymns recommended in this book. It would be hard to better this series for primary hymns.

Festivals by Jean Gilbert (Oxford University Press, Music Department, Walton Street, Oxford OX2 6DP) is a very useful anthology with suggestions for songs and musical activities related to festivals.